OCEAN VIEW CHURCH OF CHRIST
9612 - 26th BAY STREET
NORFOLK, VIRGINIA 23518

THE HOUSE

of ACTS

The House of Acts

by

John A. MacDonald

Creation House
Carol Stream, Illinois

THE HOUSE OF ACTS © 1970 by Creation House. All rights reserved. Printed in the United States of America. No part of this book may be reproduced in any manner whatsoever without permission except in the case of brief quotations embodied in reviews. For information, address Creation House, Inc., Publishers, 429 East St. Charles Road, P.O. Box 316, Carol Stream, Illinois 60187.

FIRST EDITION

Library of Congress Catalog Card Number: 70-139782

People ask: "How does your wife feel about

this ministry?"

And I answer: "No partner has been so understanding

and helpful as she."

Gratefully and lovingly, this book is dedicated to

MARILYN

CONTENTS

FOREWORD

The events related in this book are given from one perspective—my own. I trust that the telling shows that I did not make or dominate this scene. Despite the high degree of first person accounting, I am conscious of being just a small part of something that is big—far bigger than any of the many people now participating.

I want to acknowledge here the fine spirit and help of the great people who have allowed me to write about them. Their family names have been omitted from the account because, as will be seen, there are some details that could prove embarrassing. My intent is to help rather than hurt.

Many of the best helpers are behind the scenes and don't appear in this story at all. I have made some mention of my colleagues on the Board of Directors of Evangelical Concerns, Inc., at a few points in the story. Their activity has been much greater than might appear from these brief references. I suppose they could all write their own books! One board member who is not mentioned at all is the Reverend Jack Whitesell, pastor of Bethel Temple in San Francisco. Jack served as secretary-treasurer through some of our most uncertain and demanding days. He was a great help.

My appreciation for my church and many of its understanding, concerned people could not be exaggerated. True enough, we've had to face the fact of an invading culture, one with some disagreeable characteristics, and to come to some agreement as to what our faithfulness to Christ means in these circumstances. This has cost us something in terms of human associations. But I am encouraged by the spirit I see emerging. And I am grateful for support, counsel, willingness to learn and to let me learn, and much more that First Baptist Church of Mill Valley has invested in this ministry among a new kind of young generation. For these good people and all the others I am grateful to God. "O depth of wealth, wisdom, and knowledge in God! ...... Source, Guide, and Goal of all that is—to Him be glory for ever! Amen" (Rom. 11:33-36, NEB).

John A. MacDonald
Mill Valley, Calif.
October 14, 1970

INTRODUCTION

The rambling old ranch house had once been the center of a prosperous gardening enterprise that served the homes and hotels of nearby San Francisco of another day. Now its shabby appearance contrasted with the newer homes and their well-manicured lawns that surrounded it.

But any luster which the House of Acts, as the ranch house was now known, may have lacked on the exterior, it was made up this evening by the colorful interior decor. My wife, Marilyn, and I were hardly prepared for it as we entered.

Bedecked with flowers and festooned with brilliant-colored signs and decorations, it was a marvel to behold. The crowd of young people that filled the room and spilled out into the doorways of the bedrooms and kitchen were likewise colorfully clothed.

The House of Acts was well known by its neighbors. It was one of the first so-called Christian hippie communes in the area—indeed, on the whole West Coast.

The House of Acts also was held in high regard by police

11

officials of both Novato and surrounding communities. For not only did its members cooperate with the authorities, but also officers of the law had discovered that often members of the commune had been helpful to them in handling undesirable hippie characters who had begun to frequent the area.

Especially had many parents in the Novato area come to appreciate the House of Acts for its influence on their young people who might otherwise have gone down the drain on sex, drugs, and the rest of hippie culture.

The difference was that the House of Acts was a Christian commune — outwardly hippie, but also truly Christian.

The event for which we were arriving on this particular evening was our first hippie wedding. And astonishingly enough, I, a Baptist pastor with distinctly conservative theological leanings, was to perform the ceremony.

The request had come to me that same day. Although I had insisted on my customary careful premarital counsel, we had rushed from an impromptu pizza wedding supper at the parsonage to the House of Acts for the event.

Even though I was partially prepared from nearly three years of contacts with these delightful "flower children," I was startled at the scene which greeted us. True, I had seen a variety of young men and women emerge from the most bewildering, confused and often animalistic types of backgrounds and become true children of God. And many of the incidents through which they had come had been bizarre indeed. But this wedding scene was something truly different.

The bride wore a gown which had been fashioned that day by her sisters in the commune. She stood barefoot, as did the groom, but her dress only barely covered her derriere. In fact, her long blonde hair reached almost to the bottom of her dress. Flowers laced her hair.

The groom, with tousled curly black hair and a fiercely appearing black beard, grinned widely. He wore a multi-

12

colored embroidered blouse and denims which, curiously enough, also were decorated with flowers.

But both were scrupulously clean and their clothes equally so.

Rings? Of course, but made of Indian beads.

Equally as incongruous to a normal wedding scene were the dozen children squirming about the floor in their nightgowns like a brood of tiny kittens.

The evening's experience proved to be unique. But even stranger had been the events which led us to the wedding— and so would be those that immediately followed in my involvement in this hippie scene.

These were the years in which the "straight" public was first to learn of the swelling stream of young people—usually from typical middle-and upper-middle-class homes—who were breaking tradition. Leaving homes and school, they congregated first in the Haight-Ashbury district, then in such centers as Mill Valley, Big Sur, San Diego, Palo Alto and elsewhere, to live in an amoral environment in which drugs and minor crime were the way of life.

Because my involvement in these years was with these young people, I must describe their way of life—as revolting and gruesome as it may appear—for the sake of giving an accurate picture.

My purpose, however, is not simply to tell the story, but to provide some insights into a way of life which many sociologists and psychologists insist will remain with us in different guises for years to come. For we must realize that no matter how deep the degredation, God's grace still reaches out to draw to Himself those who respond to the love of Jesus.

And as I understand the gospel, our responsibility is to continually relate that grace of God to all with whom we as believers have contact. Thus, this may not always be pleasant reading, but I trust it will be helpful.

one

Life in a Pad

The day was cool and gray. Kara Megan's straight blonde hair framed a solemn but sensitive face and fell well below her shoulders as she sauntered aimlessly along Page Street. (At this point Page Street is one block south of Ashbury and crosses Haight Street in the next block.) She was barefoot and, like many of the others lounging against the buildings or standing on the curb, she was still in her teens.

The only difference between Megan—the name she preferred to go by—and most of the others around her was that she was alone. The others traveled in groups or two by two.

But Megan always had been a loner. Also unlike most of the others along this block in the Haight-Ashbury section of San Francisco, Megan walked with her chin high. She was alone, but she was not afraid. Or was she?

Is Pat jealous of me? Megan wondered. At first the older girl had appeared so friendly. But recently she had turned cool.

Of course, Peter is as nice as ever. She shrugged. *Maybe I'm only imagining.*

She had met Peter several months earlier and had liked him. When she learned that he had been picked up on a minor charge and shipped to jail in Los Angeles, she knew she had to try to get him out.

At the Los Angeles jail she told the jailer that she had to talk to Peter about providing money for his bail.

The jailer disappeared into the cellblock. She could hear him call to Peter, "There's a pretty little girl here, come to bail you out."

"Oh! Is it Candy?" she could hear Peter's voice answer.

The jailer came back to Megan. "Are you Candy?"

"No—" she replied hesitantly.

"That guy's had too many chicks for his own good," the jailer laughed.

But he returned to the cellblock and brought out Peter. Although he was surprised, Peter appeared genuinely pleased to see Megan. She paid the necessary money for his bail and they left together for San Francisco.

Megan continued to see Peter and visited his "pad," a back porch room which he shared with his "old lady," Pat. (In hippie jargon, "old lady" means a steady mistress.)

Shortly thereafter Megan's brother announced that he was moving back to Los Angeles. When Peter heard the news, he responded quickly.

"Move in with us. We've got plenty of room."

Megan was happy in the new relationship. Peter was always kind to her, and Pat appeared to really like her. They had smoked pot and dropped acid (LSD) together. They had shared food with one another, and she offered the few toilet articles she carried in a bag over her shoulder whenever she sensed Pat had a need. To her thoughtfulness Pat had responded with similar acts of kindness. She was aware, of course, that the arrangement could become difficult. For

16

while Megan was only eighteen, she was also a child of the world.

After all, Pat had been there first. *Perhaps I should leave,* Megan reasoned.

But who can I trust? she asked herself. *Just when I think someone likes me, I discover he doesn't, or that he likes someone else better. All of life seems to be that way. Maybe this life really isn't worth living—like some on the street are saying.*

True, she had thought fleetingly of that before. But then she had taken another trip and forgotten it. Suddenly Megan stopped and stared at the window she was passing.

Inside was a picture which formed the shape of an ox yoke with letters in gaudy colors which read, "Father, forgive them, for they know not what they do."

The words burned into her mind. *They must have some religious significance,* she thought. I wonder what they mean.

Religion always had held a fascination for Megan. As she looked at the words again, she vaguely recalled her thoughts as a child.

Megan's relationship with her mother had been a fairly loving one. But her father was a loner and, although her mother appeared to love him, gradually the marriage had weakened, finally ending in divorce when Megan was thirteen.

The confused situation at home was reflected in Megan's schoolwork. She simply wouldn't apply herself. Her mother had been a teacher, her father an artist. During the time the family had remained together, they had moved frequently. This meant she had attended at least ten different schools and hence had few close friends. However, one girl had remained a special friend from the first grade through high school. As she looks back now, the sudden conclusion of that friendship—when Megan discovered her friend had

17

been deceiving her—proved a turning point in her life. To find other friends, she hung around coffee houses and learned to smoke marijuana.

At fourteen, Megan ran away from home for the first time. By the time she was seventeen she was in open rebellion at her mother's permissiveness. She had been picked up by the police several times for drug possession and use.

After Megan graduated from high school she went to live with an older brother. She secured employment with a telephone company, but held her job only two months. She dropped acid and smoked pot constantly in her search for friendship.

If her mother had been permissive, her brother was more so. He allowed Megan to bring in a black army private for cohabitation. But she tired of him and left to visit another brother in San Francisco. Here she lied her way into the same telephone company, but could hold the job only a month. Too many absences, too often stoned on the job.

Then her brother decided to return to Southern California, and the natural and simple solution was to move in with Peter. But there was a problem. Pat was there also.

But now her security was tumbling down around her. It was clear that Pat was jealous; she wanted Peter for herself. Because she was so sensitive, Megan could understand how Pat felt.

Is there no other way to find friendship? she asked as she stared numbly at the sign in the store window.

Megan looked at the words again. Slowly she read, "Father, forgive them, for they know not what they do." She pushed open the door.

Megan was unprepared for what she found. The former store space was long and narrow. Unlike many similar storefronts in the area, however, it appeared clean. No rubbish on the floor. And the walls—festooned with graffiti aplenty—but different. Whirls and scrolls and words—words about Jesus and God.

Timidly Megan looked around. They were the same sort of people: barefoot, shaggy-haired, some with beards. But they appeared different. Several even smiled at her.

"Have some coffee?" a tall blond with a drooping moustache invited.

"Doughnuts too," he said.

Gratefully she moved toward a long table at the end of the room where others were lounging.

"Ted's my name," the blond said, holding out the cup.

She thanked him and picked out the smallest doughnut.

A girl took her feet from the chair and pushed it toward her. She sat down and looked around.

The blond moustache sat down beside her. "You've been around for some time," he said. "I've seen you on the street."

She searched his eyes for a clue. Was he a pusher, or did he just have a pad he wanted to share? Puzzled, she could see nothing.

"Yes," she said, lowering her eyes, "I have. But I may not be here much longer."

"Oh," was the reply. "Here, meet Sarah."

Megan looked up to the friendly smile of a girl with long dark hair. She slid into the chair that Ted had vacated.

"I'd like you to meet Joe and Judy," she said, nodding to a boy and girl across the table. Both smiled, and Megan wondered vaguely how it could be that so many pleasant people were gathered in one place.

"More coffee?" a dark, curly haired boy with a full beard asked. She nodded, and he began to pour. Somehow Megan felt she had never had so much kindness extended toward her before.

"What is this place?" she asked.

"We call it the Living Room," replied Sarah.

When she left an hour later, Megan knew that she would be back — and not just for the coffee and doughnuts — but for the friendship she had sensed among those whom she had met. She didn't understand their talk about Jesus, but she was vaguely aware that she wanted to. Maybe this was the answer to her problem.

Megan walked for another two hours, stopping occasionally to talk to persons whom she had seen somewhere before. But there was nothing to talk about, so she moved on. By late afternoon she was back at the community house. As she climbed the stairs, she could hear voices.

Who can that be? she wondered. Turning the corner, she was totally unprepared for the greeting.

"Hi! You again," came the cheerful voice of the black-bearded boy whom she had met that morning in the Living Room.

"Hullo," Megan replied. She was surprised to realize how pleased she was to see him again. Usually one boy had made no more difference than another. That is—except Peter.

"I'm telling Pat and Peter about Jesus," Rick said. "Sit down and rap with us."

Megan noticed that Pat moved slightly to offer her space on the mattress. But she did not look up.

"Thanks," murmured Megan, "maybe I'll listen."

In the days that followed Megan saw more and more of Rick, Ted and the others. Either they came to the community house to talk to Peter about Jesus, or she would go with Peter and Pat to the Living Room. Here the men would concentrate on Peter, reading from the Bible or talking at length about Jesus and their faith in Him.

The more she listened, the more convinced Megan became that she must come someday to know Jesus—like Rick and the others. But not now. She was too young, and life was too interesting—that is, so long as there was enough pot or LSD to go around.

two

Rebellion Begins Early

In many ways my invitation to perform the unusual wedding at the House of Acts proved a climax to my encounters with young men and women on the hippie scene over a period of more than three years.

Certainly I was deeply touched at the wedding by the groom's remark, "I think of you as a father."

I was honored to be so accepted by him, as I have been by many of the other flower children. But this acceptance was not handed out carelessly. Neither did I win it easily. In fact, I look back with chagrin at my many blunders. Not only did I often err, but too frequently have I been thoughtless—even selfish and proud—in my unwillingness to comprehend the miracle of God which has opened before me.

Certainly I deserve no credit for what God has done. In fact, I did not even initiate the first contact with these young people who deserted the institutional society and found the reality of the living God through a personal relationship with Jesus Christ, totally apart from the organized church.

My first contact came when a girl named Liz appeared one Sunday morning in our church service. Later her mother visited me and, quietly, but with obvious deep anxiety, pleaded with me to visit Liz's home and do what I could. Without giving details, she implied difficulties existed. That was familiar news. I knew a mother's concern doesn't often match that of the next generation, but I agreed to call.

A few days later I visited with Liz and discovered that she possessed a clear, articulate faith in Jesus Christ. I urged her to attend our services regularly with her family, and to unite with our church. She told me about her husband with warm affection, but she didn't actually relate anything of Ted's troubles.

"Is he a Christian?" I asked.

She hesitated only momentarily. "No, but he's going to be."

"Then I hope to see him in church soon," I said. At the same time I made a mental note that I must meet Ted soon. This I did—but the real facts of his life I did not learn until long afterward. Their revelation opened a whole new world to me and our church.

When he was seven years old, Ted moved with his family from his birthplace at Clearlake, across the state of California to Auburn, one of the old gold-trail towns of the Sierra foothills. Situated on a major cross-country highway, it has survived much better than most of the gold-mining towns of a ghosted era.

With older and younger brother and a half sister, Ted grew up in that community which could be described as one of the more wholesome environments for a boy to know. But his parents, economically stable and reasonably happy together, never attended church. Their children were never taken or even sent to Sunday school. The only time Ted ever recalls having been in a church was when his grandmother took him to Sunday school in the small town of Upper Lake when he was still very young.

In Auburn, Ted completed high school and one semester

of Sierra College, one of California's numerous public junior colleges. Then he went into the navy. He insists that he entered as an extremely patriotic youth who sincerely believed that the military service offered noble fulfillment for true young Americans. He finished training as a seaman first-class and was assigned to a repair ship which sailed for Japan.

Disillusionment followed. The navy did not provide any sense of patriotic fulfillment. In reaction, his aggressive intelligence soon taught him the art of hustling. (A hustler is a person who uses his wits to procure, by fair means or foul, goods or services for sale.) A hustler is a sort of underworld entrepreneur. Ted was a good one.

He made friends with a boatswain hustler who was otherwise unliked aboard ship. The bos'n first managed to get Ted transferred to the sail loft, where he taught him the rudiments of the sail-making trade. The skill enabled him to do favors for superiors, such as mending clothes and sewing insignia on uniforms. In return he was given more personal privileges than anyone else on board. He had little duty and much liberty.

With the loss of his patriotic fervor, Ted became conscious of a vague hunger for an emotional or ethereal experience. At a Japanese port, a group of Japanese musicians helped fill the vacuum. They were taking heroin and introduced its use to Ted and a shipmate. The heroin was strong, pure stuff, not diluted as is the ordinary United States supply. Injecting this narcotic was exciting. Ted and his friend vied with one another to see who could be the first and highest. They didn't bother to work up gradually, but began at the top, paying for their indulgence with horrible wretching and visual interference.

The ship moved to another port where no heroin was available. But on return to Yokosuka they once again contacted the musicians and began injecting heroin every night. From all appearances they were hooked.

When his ship was scheduled to return to the United States, Ted tried to transfer to another ship in the harbor in order to stay close to his heroin supply. The transfer did not come through until he arrived back in the United States, however. So he flew back to Japan and his destiny with dope.

The lack of privacy aboard ship forced a measure of restraint, but somehow they managed to live continuously on the "Big H."

When his ship moved to another port, Ted was separated from the important supply. But a shipmate soon located a Korean Communist junkee for a connection. The group was caught and given suspended sentences following trial and conviction. As a result, Ted was transferred back to the United States and separated from the service.

Returning home, he enrolled at Sierra College. He worked tending bar and kept fairly straight. But one day an old friend just out of service came along with a heroin connection. Ted turned on again, racing with his friend to be first and highest on smack.

At this time romance entered Ted's life in the form of Liz, a slim, dark-haired girl who had turned rebel while in her teens. Liz's parents were active in the First Baptist Church and, while she was a child, had helped her make her profession in Christ. She had been baptized, but even as a youth her willful nature got her into trouble.

By the time she had reached her early teens, Liz had thrown off all restraints of both home and church. Ted's swashbuckling characteristics proved attractive to Liz, several years his junior.

But Auburn was too small for Liz and her quest for fortune; she left for San Francisco. Ted followed and enrolled at a school of arts and crafts. By the time he arrived on the scene, he was astonished to discover what an able hustler Liz had become in the big city.

For ambitious Liz, marriage had no place at this point.

She enjoyed her modeling job and delighted in matching wits with others. In her own mind she was not ready for the responsibilities of either husband or children.

But Ted was ever present and always persistent. Soon she was dismayed to discover she was pregnant. Despite their wayward ways, the two possessed a strong sense of rightness; so they were married and moved into the O'Farrell Street House, a commune operated out of North Beach by a beatnik who was also a Zen Buddhist. Here they found speed freaks who injected methadrene into their veins. The drug was cheap and easily available through the willing cooperation of a woman doctor who hoped to cure heroin addicts by getting them on methadrene. Speed freaks and amphetamines subsequently became the big dope traffic in San Francisco—and another serious problem to health and safety.

Up to this time Ted and Liz had been going fairly straight. But the cost of taking speed now forced Ted back to hustling with its illegal activity. Then a friend arrived with information on how to secure peyote for ten dollars a supply via a mail-order subterfuge. Peyote brought Ted to some clearer awareness of his spiritual thirst and ignorance at first; but when the government moved in on the mail-order house, he was forced to return to dexodrene.

Into this confused scene a baby daughter, Erin, was born on July 28, 1961. Now hustling was not enough to keep Ted in school and put food on the table for his wife and child. He dropped out of school and the family moved to Sausalito where he secured employment as a sailmaker. He conned a doctor into giving him a prescription for dexodrene to be refilled indefinitely.

By now a sense of futility with his way of life was grow- ing on Ted. Marital problems developed, for Liz, with her supressed faith and strong Christian background, was becoming increasingly unhappy.

Then an old friend of Ted's from Auburn by the name of

Dan arrived in town, bringing marijuana, popularly known as pot or grass. The drug came into common use in Ted's home. By then the first publicity had begun to center on the Haight-Ashbury scene, and Ted and Dan shared some of the first black-market LSD taken in San Francisco. The hippie scene was beginning to emerge. Acid heads and speed freaks were moving between Berkeley and Haight-Ashbury, seemingly expecting "something to happen."

At the same time, Liz began to attend our church, though erratically. What we didn't know then was that often she came while high on acid. One Sunday when she attended our women's Sunday school class and the teacher asked if there were any special requests for prayer, Liz said simply,

"Please pray for my husband."

We noted Liz's generally sad countenance but, regrettably, none of us realized the depths of despair and sin with which she and Ted were struggling. On his part, Ted was doing his best to talk Liz out of her childhood faith. And her willingness to share with him the tragic life of drugs and hustling made him feel his efforts were successful.

But God had not given up His child.

Ted had smoked grass or marijuana as far back as his navy days in San Diego. But it never became a serious factor in his life until reintroduced by Dan. Now he and Liz began to use it regularly. Most hippies considered it a source of pleasant relaxation. Our group of Christian flower children has come to regard it as clearly a dangerous drug because of the ease with which users move from it to more powerful narcotics or hallucinogens.

LSD or "acid" was new on the scene then. Ted rationalized himself into becoming an acid head as a phase of his futile search for reality which lasted for two and a half years.

Ted says that the first sharp insight he had to his real self came through LSD trips. "Trip" is an accurate description of the experience. During the drug state, the user becomes strangely detached so that he appears to view himself objectively from a distance. However, the repeated experience also shows that after "coming down," the memory of what was seen remains. But there is no will or ability to do anything about it. Hence, Ted saw himself as a liar, a cheat, a vile self-centered sinner. But once off a trip, and even realizing a need for reform, the problem loomed too large and great to handle.

Ted did make repeated efforts at reformation because he knew his life was all wrong, and that his wife and family deserved a better break. But all efforts proved futile. Rationalization helped. He also adopted the hippie philosophy of giving up possessions to help others. But still the continued revelation of his sin via LSD trips gave him no peace.

About this time also Ted took to asserting his personal freedom in defiance of accepted moral codes. He went to one mistress after another, and at one time was in adulterous relationship with five different women. Liz was suspicious of what was going on, but her only course of action was to join him on LSD trips.

One night Ted was on his way to San Rafael to visit one of his mistresses. Entering the freeway, his eyes fell upon a recently erected sign. "Go back!" it read. "You're going the wrong way."

That, with many other signs—both real and imagined—continually screamed at him about the wrongness of his life. But he had no spiritual strength to change. Clearly he was moving toward the brink of destruction and, despite himself, was dragging his family with him.

One danger with LSD is that the user never knows how much he is getting because it is poorly measured. A great variety of experiences may result, including temporary schizophrenia or paranoia and even a catatonic extreme. The feeling of being on a trip, users say, is incredible. The drug makes you think you are learning something, but later

27

this proves to be a delusion. Then the user begins wondering what is really happening. He longs for someone to step in and tell him whether or not this is good. His retreat is into a terrible subjectivity. No one else is present or in view; he may even think himself to be God. But he has no way to discern what is right and wrong; and he can't tell whether he is hallucinating. Despair and suicide often result because the poor acid head has no defense against what is emotionally painful and always present.

Amazingly enough, despite this situation in the home, Ted began reading the Bible. Indoctrinated in the hippie insistence on love, he knew the Bible had something to say on that subject. He had no faith that it was God's Word. In fact, he was sure it was hopelessly corrupt. What he did find there of Christian ethics he interpreted to support his own behavior. In effect, he was right and everyone else was wrong.

Yet, strangely and wonderfully, the Word of God managed to penetrate his defenses. Gradually a conviction of sin became clear in his mind. He understood Christ's claims to be Lord, and the importance of acknowledging Him.

He also recognized his own lack of personal power to handle his problems. And, actually, in spite of romanticizing his ten years of drug use, he came to understand he had never really trusted dope. He realized he had been looking for a way out of the world rather than a way to handle life.

At this juncture he came to believe that Christ was able to save him from the consequences of his present life which had come to pose a serious threat. The moment came when Ted simply prayed and asked Jesus Christ to save him. Seeking assurance that he was really saved, he found meaning in the scriptural command to confess Christ publicly. He resolved to do this among the people he knew best.

Without sharing his conviction with Liz, he arranged for both of them to drive to a friend's home in Berkeley where he meant to make his public profession. But before leaving he "copped out," and both he and Liz took acid. Then they got in their car to drive to Berkeley.

On the way he told Liz, "I'm going to do something very difficult tonight."

"You're always doing that," she chided.

"If I do, will you stick with me?" he asked.

"But what are you going to do?" Liz pressed.

But Ted could only shake his head. It was his decision, he knew, but he couldn't share it with Liz. Not yet, anyway.

They were welcomed at the friend's home where many hippies were coming and going. All were smoking grass and were high. But Ted and Liz were the only ones present who had taken LSD, a fact which Liz happened to let slip. (This proved to be an embarrassment since those who take LSD usually don't do so when others are smoking grass.) This left them somewhat out of harmony with the rest of the group, and again, Ted was overcome with fear.

How can I possibly make my confession of Jesus Christ in such an atmosphere? he reasoned.

At the same time, however, he could feel the acid taking effect. Knowing he would soon be "stoned," he became desperate. A lull suddenly came in the conversation and everyone was quiet.

Into the stillness Ted's normally soft voice boomed:

"Jesus is my Lord and Savior."

Stunned, cold silence filled the room. Now Ted had no alternative, it seemed to him; he and Liz must leave. But by this time they were in no condition to drive anywhere— much less on the freeway on a Saturday night. But onto the Bay Bridge toward San Francisco they went. All along the way Ted could hear voices which shouted, "Flee! Flee! Flee!"

He did not understand what they were or meant. He was convinced that he had stopped the car right in the middle of the Bay Bridge, midway between Oakland and San Francisco, too stoned to go on. Liz sat quietly at his side,

29

totally incapable of helping. In desperation he prayed, "Lord, help! Help us, Lord!"

In this strange and weird period, Ted could not see clearly. Then he became vaguely aware that he was still driving and that cars were passing on both sides. He wanted to stop the car and to get out, but he asserts that the Lord told him not to do so.

LSD does strange things, such as making a person feel he is in two places at the same time. Simultaneously, Ted had felt he was driving, but also that he had parked the car and was walking.

Liz says she was dimly cognizant of the fact that he was rocking back and forth over the steering wheel in obvious agitation. One thing Ted is sure of: his conversations with Jesus Christ that night were real.

"I will get you home safely and will save you," He said.

Several times Ted claims he tried to get out of the car, but the Lord stopped him.

"No, you must stay in the car and keep driving."

When Ted attempted to argue, the Lord replied, "I am going to save you. But you must go to church, and you must speak My words to everyone."

"What can I say?" Ted asked.

"You are to say, 'He is back.' Nothing more," was the reply.

Ted had never attended church as an adult. He was convinced that only hypocrites did so, and that church people were hopelessly institutionalized and out of touch with the real world. This is the way he thought about it the morning after their safe arrival at home.

Since being stoned on LSD means you don't sleep, Ted hadn't. This gave him plenty of time to rationalize the events of the evening before. Thus by 10 o'clock Sunday morning Ted had fairly well ruled out the possibility of attending church.

Then the telephone rang. A male voice with a Texas

accent asked for an unknown person. Ted gave the usual reply, "Wrong number," and put down the phone.

Then he became convicted. "That was the first person I have spoken to today and Jesus told me last night to say, 'He is back' to everyone with whom I spoke."

Frantically, Ted asked God for another opportunity.

"I'll say what You told me to say. Just give me another chance," he pleaded.

Hardly had the prayer been uttered when the phone rang again. The same man asked for the same unknown person. This time Ted was ready.

"He's not here—but He is back!" he said.

"Well," replied the Texas voice, "I guess I won't have to call anymore today."

Now Ted was determined he must go to church. He and Liz appeared together, and that morning when the invitation was given, Ted quickly stood up, and with a smile made the simple assertion,

"He is back."

To this day Ted cannot explain the "He is back" thing except to relate it to the fact that it helped free him from fear of being seen as a fool.

In the weeks that followed, Ted went through the prescribed course of instruction leading to baptism. This began with private sessions with me. My recollection of that beginning is of dealing with a person who was genuinely changed in attitude, and most certainly a believer in Jesus Christ. He was honestly ignorant, but most eager to learn. Curiously enough, his baptism was unavoidably postponed for several weeks because of a leak in our baptistry. Ted became restless over the delay; now he regards it as pure providence. For to him baptism was to be another way of getting high—so much a part of his life had that type of experience become.

Watching the growth of these two young people, and the development of their family life into a full-blown center of genuine love and affection as well as deep devotion to the Lord, was a rare privilege for me.

What I didn't realize was that this was only the beginning of a vast, new and exciting experience for me, Marilyn, and our whole church membership.

three

The Swinging Set

Maybe we at the First Baptist Church of Mill Valley were naïve in those days. But I don't think so. What was happening was that the hippie scene, which was later to get such widespread publicity both in the San Francisco area and around the world, was just emerging. We weren't prepared for it and hence did not recognize it.

Ted's family occupied a modest flat close to his work. His hair was no longer than many men's hair, and even his bushy sandy-colored moustache was not unusual. His clothes were mod but not ridiculous. Liz commonly wore simple short dresses, and her hair was straight and of moderate length. The children were tastefully dressed and clean.

Put such a family in an arty community in a liberal sector of California, and add to this picture the fact that the term *hippie* would not become common for another year, and the reasons for our ignorance may become clear. Plainly, Ted and Liz and their friends had moved in the circle of young rebels during that formative period when the hippie thing

33

emerged which we knew nothing about. They were actually pre-hippies and, in a sense, did not themselves go into the later much-publicized negative movement. Yet, they were close to it and quite able to converse meaningfully with those caught up in the scene.

Moreover, Ted and Liz immediately gave up the use of LSD, grass and other drugs. We simply assumed they were following a normal course of events.

However, after about a year of abstinence, Ted became convinced that he should take another LSD trip to see if it would be the same. It wasn't. For the first time he became aware of the presence of demons. This convinced him of the impropriety of the use of drugs on the part of Christians. The sensation was the same — of being apart from oneself or split. This time he recognized and dismissed the illusions he experienced, for he knew that in reality he possessed his strong Christian convictions and that the heart of these convictions was the reality of the Word of God complementing the Holy Spirit of God.

I was not aware of his "tripping-out" again at the time, but I did become aware of Ted's increasingly active witness of his faith. He was convinced beyond a shadow of a doubt that he had something far better, far more satisfying and stabilizing. And this was the only *high* he needed.

Ted by nature is a strong, intelligent and aggressive person. If his early forays into the exciting arenas of heroin and LSD were not his most intelligent acts, they at least demonstrate his activism. He had spent ten years in a feverish search for meaning in life. And when Christ came and brought understanding and peace, Ted did not lie down and go to sleep.

Real life was just beginning, and Ted was joyously aware of it. His face radiated the thrill of his discovery. He punctuated our first conversations with exclamations of wonder at the "incredible" thing that had happened to him. Far from exhibiting any uncertainty as to where he stood with God, or where he could find a place as a Christian, he plunged into the new life with irrepressible zest.

I am sure that, even with all of his natural capacity for trying something new, he had never before tackled anything with a spirit to match this new start. He was a sprinter taking off with a crack of the starter's gun. He was a gourmet entering a king's feast. But more. He knew he had taken nearly thirty years to reach this climactic encounter, and he wasn't about to waste any more time getting to work.

The stream of young people who had previously frequented Ted and Liz's apartment to smoke marijuana and talk about the endless subjects of hippie life now became objects of Ted's prayer and concern. Jim was the first to respond.

Jim and his wife, Judy, with their daughter, Jennifer, moved to California from Des Moines, Iowa, in 1961. Friends since kindergarten days, Steve and his wife, Sandi, followed in 1965.

According to Jim, he grew up in what he identifies as an average Christian home. The family attended church regularly but didn't consistently practice their faith at home.

Jim claims he had no idea of what it meant to personally trust Jesus Christ. When he met Judy, however, he found a girl who knew what she believed and who needed spiritual companionship. To keep in with her he told her he had been religious at one time.

A stage career was Jim's ambition. He had completed more than two years of work in three different colleges in the Midwest, majoring in speech and drama.

Judy, on the other hand, had made a genuine commitment to Christ at the age of fourteen and had a strong desire to become fully involved in Christian activity. Her homelife had been a happy one and family relationships were close. Hers was an upper-middle-class environment, however, where social position played a large part in the large Presbyterian church which the family attended. Judy's parents refused to be hypocritical about their Saturday night social life, and therefore seldom attended church.

As one of the church's youth, however, Judy was given spiritual attention. Her church sent her to summer camps and retreats. Thus the need to make personal commitment to Christ was made clear. On one memorable trip to a missionary conference in Pennsylvania there was born in her a zeal for missionary service.

This commitment Judy never forgot. Nor did she cease praying that the Lord would provide her with that opportunity. But sidestep it she did. At seventeen she began to open up her life to sub-Christian activity and for several years she went through mental agony. She feared for her own sanity but kept on praying. Despite those rocky times, in September, 1959, Judy and Jim were married.

Judy held the hope that sometime she and Jim would work together for the Lord. She managed to get him to join her in evening Bible reading for their first three months together, but Jim's interest soon flagged.

Marriage meant dropping out of school for Jim, but he had no trouble securing a well-paying position. Their first daughter, Jennifer, was born in April of 1961 while they were still in Des Moines. The beginning of their own family would seemingly have brought happiness to a couple able to make out as well as Jim and Judy. But Jim was restless and wanted to make his try in the entertainment world. By this time Judy had become disillusioned with churches and church people. But still sensing her need for spiritual fellowship, and especially in times of uncertainty, she continued to pray alone.

Then came the move to California. Work here was not easily found, and when Jim did land a nightclub spot as a comedian the results proved disastrous. Meanwhile, a second baby was on the way; Julie was born on July 17, 1963.

The nightclub job washed out soon and Jim wound up as a tobacco salesman. While this provided a more stable income, it did not satisfy his urge for a more dramatic life.

36

The result, curiously enough, was that Jim dived into political activity, identifying himself with extreme conservative causes. Although he sympathized with the John Birch Society, he did not join that group simply because he feared possible harm to his stage ambitions. At the same time, he became aware of a spiritual hunger which, because he was unwilling to identify it as such, he never took too many pains to satisfy.

About this time Jim began to entertain sexual fantasies. This led to several adulterous relationships and, in order to justify his actions, he encouraged Judy to do the same. This was not her inclination, but in an effort to conform to his way of life she did so. To her astonishment, Jim became jealous.

In order to find a way out of the dilemma which he did not recognize as his own making, Jim decided that he and Judy should join the Sexual Freedom League. They went to only one party. What they saw so frightened them that they never returned.

In spite of these aberrations, Jim and Judy maintained something of a happy family life. Their children were accepted, and genuine love was shared in the family. They had what was good, but thought that the greatest good in life was to conform to the world around them.

Jim tried hard to be the self-sufficient man. But at Thanksgiving, 1965, he overreached himself. With fourteen friends seated around a well-supplied table, Jim arose with his drink in hand to make a speech.

"God is dead," he said with a thick tongue. "You can thank me for the feast laid before you."

Judy was horified and ran into the kitchen, crying. Angered, Jim followed.

"What are you trying to do—embarrass me?" he shouted angrily.

"But you don't know what you said," replied Judy tearfully.

37

At that Jim struck her sharply across the mouth. Judy staggered to the corner of the kitchen, sobbing.

Nothing seemed to be able to stop Jim's downward path. Like many other young people in the hippie scene, or on the fringe of it, in those days, he quit drinking and began to smoke pot. Like others of the turned-on generation, he became exhilarated with its effects and was ready for other drugs as soon as they appeared. LSD came next. By this time Judy had become terrified and seriously considered divorcing her husband.

But God indeed was not dead. He had not given up on Jim. Somehow Judy's prayers began to have their effect. In the year that followed the momentous Thanksgiving scene, a sense of personal guilt emerged in Jim's mind and heart. It appeared as though his fit of atheism had triggered a genuine fright of the possibility of God's reality.

Jim and Judy had kept in regular touch with Steve and Sandi, their longtime Des Moines friends, through the years. And one evening they went with them to visit Ted and Liz.

Liz and Sandi had met at a nursery school sometime before. When Sandi and Steve had invited Liz and Ted to their home, a Sausalito penthouse which a variety of hippie and near-hippie types frequented, Steve had been impressed by the two. Instead of arguing the standard political views, they had merely said, "We are Christians."

The two couples had visited several times, but this was Jim's first direct exposure to Ted. He was fascinated, and listened intently while Ted and Steve engaged in an earnest conversation about the person of Jesus Christ.

"For the first time in my life I saw the sinfulness of my life," he says now.

Suddenly the thought struck him: Maybe there is a God.

No sooner had this idea come to him then he discovered that he was breathing freely and easily—a sensation which he had not had for some time. Then, while the others continued their conversation, Jim retired quietly to the sanc-

38

tuary of his own heart and prayed, "God, forgive me."

At that moment, Jim now avows, he knew he was a free man.

It took another two months before he came to understand about the person of Jesus Christ and His place in his new life. But he had many long discussions with Ted, and together the two talked and read the Bible. Judy, of course, was also a great help to him, and it wasn't long before they came to our church for the first time.

During this period Ted and Liz had kept us informed of their conversation with the different characters in their hippie world. Giving their first names only, they would ask us to pray for them. This we did. But had we fully known the wild and woolly world toward which we, the pastor and members of the First Baptist Church of Mill Valley, were moving, I am sure we would have been apprehensive.

four

Even the "Good" Can Fall

Those of us who were straight people in the greater San Francisco area were becoming aware that we were being caught in a vortex of a new and strange way of living.

Hippie life, as it had become known around the world, centered in that bleak part of the city whose vacant storefronts and low-cost rooming houses afforded a quick sanctuary for young people of an affluent society looking for a thrill. For the most part they came from middle-class to affluent homes. They lacked nothing—but a challenge to live for. Not finding it in their home, school or church life, they sought it elsewhere. Somehow or another, the corner of Haight and Ashbury Streets became a symbol to them of the freedom from restraint for which they were looking.

Steve and Sandi followed in this train, although by this time they were married and the parents of one child, and were somewhat older. Coming from the Middle West, they had followed their childhood friends, Jim and Judy, because of the excitement they expected to find.

According to Steve, his mother was a true believer in Jesus Christ. She taught him in the Scriptures when he was a child and also sent him to Sunday school, not going herself because his father objected. But Steve recalls that his mother attended prayer meetings at the church when his father was away on business.

From this otherwise normal homelife, Steve enrolled at Drake University. Here he became a journalism major, specializing in radio. University life proved to be a ball. Steve thoroughly enjoyed his studies and was popular with his fellow students. Then in his junior year he met Sandra, a slim brunette from Chicago.

Picking her up at her sorority house on one of their first dates, he announced solemnly, "You are going to marry me."

Sandra's response was to hoot with laughter. And probably with good reason. She had come to Drake University from her home in a Chicago suburb where whe had been the center of attention and where life had offered her everything she desired. Why should she give up all this so soon to be married to a man and to do his bidding? This wasn't her idea of how to enjoy life.

As a result of Sandi's attitude, the romance rocked along for the next few years. Many times it appeared doomed, only to be revived again on the next date.

Sandi had grown up in a strong Irish Catholic home in Chicago. As she describes it, her childhood was "beautiful."

She was the oldest in her family, and there, as well as among her cousins, she enjoyed the spotlight. The parish priest was a good family friend and visited the home often. Her good mind and outgoing personality won her popularity in the parochial school which she attended. In addition, she was twice named a "quiz kid" on a popular Chicago radio program.

When the family moved to a suburb, however, her lifestyle was threatened. Although classes in the new parochial school were smaller, Sandi found the situation more competitive. As a result, she withdrew into herself, began to put on weight and, by the time she had reached the eighth grade, was seriously considering becoming a nun.

At this juncture her father, realizing something needed to be done, stepped into the picture. He didn't like the separation of sexes which characterized that particular parochial education, and insisted that Sandi go to a public school. She became the only girl of her eighth grade graduating class to do so. At first embarrassed, she came to realize and appreciate her father's decision.

In high school Sandi's truer self surfaced; she blossomed again into a free, outgoing spirit. She entered the university with great expectations and was not disappointed. Pledging a sorority her first year, she made good grades throughout her university career and, as she says, "had a marvelous time."

The stormy campus courtship came to a climax in 1960. After graduation Sandi and Steve were married in what she describes as a "picture book wedding."

Sandi's "ideal life" continued true to form when within their first year of marriage their first child, Steven, was born. But the picture did not hold true to form for long. The three additional children she desired, spaced at the proper intervals, did not arrive. Moreover, the girl who had had everything discovered she was married to a strong-minded man, and that her destiny was now tied to his. The girl who had always managed to have her own way realized that she was in a different and troublesome position.

In 1963 the young family moved to Milwaukee, Wisconsin, where Steve realized his first solid success in radio broadcasting. He took the name of Steve O'Shea in order to better advance his career. Two years later Steve moved his wife and son to San Francisco.

The name of Steve O'Shea quickly caught on at radio station KNBR, a powerful San Francisco NBC outlet. Life in the entertainment world in San Francisco moved at a fast pace. Steve and Sandi took a penthouse in Sausalito which was soon frequented by the so-called "beautiful people" of the entertainment industry as well as by the bizarre hippies who by then were in full swing.

In this scene, liquor became old hat, and drugs the "in" thing. For a period of nine months Steve, who never had a drinking problem, experimented with LSD and pot. Sandi became frightened. She opposed the use of drugs in their home. But Steve laid down the law.

"I'm looking for a spiritual experience," he asserted. "You can either go along or get out."

"But why don't we go back to church?" she pleaded.

"Ridiculous!" he exploded. "You know as well as I that church has nothing to offer."

Ruefully, Sandi admitted Steve was right. Vaguely she thought of looking into other churches than her own. But she dismissed the thought; it was easier to go along with Steve. And strangely, taking drugs made it possible for her to overlook what she had come to suspect: there were other women in Steve's life.

Meanwhile, Sandi could not shake the image of her devout father. She cannot remember a night passing when he was not on his knees in prayer. And he was always on hand for daily mass. But by this time Sandi no longer attended church, and hardly considered herself a Roman Catholic. This pleased Steve. He could see only hypocrisy and human error in the church—and especially in the Roman Catholic church.

About this time Steve and Sandi suffered the first visible shock from their way of life. They had taken a baby girl, Susan, into their home with the hope of adopting her. One day the social caseworker called to ask routine questions relative to their care of Susan.

"Are you still a practicing Roman Catholic?" she asked.

"No," replied Sandi truthfully.

44

"Are you taking drugs?"

Again Sandi replied honestly, "Yes."

"Oh! Well, that's too bad, because in that case we have no choice but to take Susan out of your home."

Meanwhile, more trouble crowded into their fast-paced life. Steve's career, which had been on a meteoric ascendency, had run into trouble. After fourteen months at KNBR, he had moved to KFRC as both a disc jockey and as emcee of a talk show. The move had brought more exciting people into his life. Now he and his pal Jim added gambling to their present pastime of finding new girls to bed down with.

At KFRC Steve attained the highest disc jockey rating in the area with the public, but not with the station manager.

"You talk too much about yourself," the manager complained.

"Look, how do you think I keep my rating?" Steve objected.

But the station manager had the last word, and Steve was dumped from his disc jockey position.

As they look back now, Sandi and Steve are not sure whether it was this combination of events alone which led to their next big decision, or whether it was simply a desire to try a different life-style more in keeping with the restless and unsettled period through which they were going. At any rate, they suddenly gave up their beautiful new home which they had occupied only a few months before and moved in with their old-time midwestern friends, Judy and Jim. This was the spring of 1967.

By this time Jim was frantically reading the Bible, discoursing long and earnestly with Liz and Ted on the subject of the Christian life and his newfound faith in Jesus Christ. Also, Jim had cut off his extramarital activity. Although still on the prowl, Steve had narrowed his down to the friendly bed he had discovered in his secretary's apartment.

As for Sandi, she had gone through a pantheistic period

in her thinking. But through her use of drugs she had come at least to realize that she couldn't be a god herself. Regrettably, however, she didn't want the Christ she knew to be God. Indeed, she very much liked the freedom she had found in becoming a dropout from Roman Catholicism, but she had to admit that the freedom had not brought happiness.

Judy, the secret believer, was simply keeping quiet.

One thing appears abundantly clear. In all of this, the Holy Spirit was moving inexorably to draw both Sandi and Steve to a personal relationship with Christ.

Under the bombardment of Jim's Bible reading and the conversations with him and Ted, Steve knew he had to make some sort of a move. He became convinced that the life he was leading spelled only hopeless misery. Although he couldn't quite comprehend the love of Christ, he did become aware of his sin. In desperation he determined to break off his adulterous relationship with his secretary.

"At least God will know I am trying," he reasoned.

God responded, revealing His love to Steve. And the finest fruit of Steve's decision was his own wife's salvation. For in a few weeks, clearly realizing her deep personal need, Sandi too received Jesus Christ as her Lord and Savior.

The results were immediate.

Steve in his own way found new release and zest for his radio talent. He now began a daily three-hour disc jockey program on radio station KYA in San Francisco. Here he freely witnessed to his new life in Christ, and the program brought quick response. The station manager reacted to the religious approach by bouncing Steve from the program, but this had little effect on his spiritual life. From their comfortable living of recent years, the family was now being led into a day-to-day subsistence with their close friends, none working regularly, but all feeling compelled to give their time to a personal witness for Christ among their hippie friends.

Sandi summed it up: "Ever since childhood I've had the

feeling that some day I would be involved in something special. School, marriage, children—all of these were wonderful—but none was fully satisfying. Steve and I agree we never found real peace until we discovered the real Person, Jesus Christ. And the wonderful part about it is that we are both in Him together."

By the time of the conversion of Jim and Judy and Steve and Sandi, I was beginning to see the picture. The young men and women who were peopling our neighborhood were a different breed from those we had known before. In many cases they may have had a traditional background, but usually this background played a small part in the contemporary world in which they lived and moved.

And if we wished to minister to these young people, it began to occur to me, some adjustments might have to be made in our own way of thinking. Certainly in mine.

five

Morality Adrift

One more link remained to be forged before the Lord could bring together a team of young people, early on the hippie scene, and ready to witness to their newfound faith in Christ at the height of the hippie life in the Haight-Ashbury section of San Francisco.

I had been aware of Ted and Liz's witness to their non-conformist friends in only a vague sort of way. Admittedly, I had been somewhat fearful because I knew this meant they were moving in circles where the smoking of pot, the dropping of acid, and the use of other drugs, as well as promiscuous sex, was a normal way of life. But because Liz and Ted appeared to be making good progress in their spiritual lives themselves, I could only murmur approval as Ted urged us to pray for this person or that.

Then one Sunday morning Ted approached me after church, evidencing unusual excitement.

"Jim has accepted Christ!" he said.

"Wonderful!" I exclaimed, "That's a real answer to prayer."

Eagerly he described how Jim had only overheard a conversation when he suddenly became aware of his sin. And by voicing the prayer of forgiveness, he had sensed the peace of God in his mind and heart.

It sounded a bit simplistic to me, but for Ted's sake I went along. Naturally I was grateful for this encouragement to Ted and sincerely hoped the conversion was real.

A week later he came with a report of another conversion, an old friend of his from college days. I was particularly grateful for this because we had been praying for Dan for months, and there had been times when Ted appeared cast into the deepest gloom because of Dan's refusal to listen.

Later, as Dan himself pieced together his story and that of his wife, Sandy, I began to see the emerging of a pattern by which the Holy Spirit was moving into the hippie community, drawing out of it those young men and young women whom He was calling to faith in Jesus Christ.

Certainly the story of Dan and Sandy's conversion might be as typical as any.

When Dan was five years old, his father joined the Marine Corps and the family moved from Flint, Michigan, to Costa Mesa, California. While Dan was taken to Sunday school by his mother, who taught a class, he was not interested and did not understand what he was being taught. His mother's gentle influence over him was somewhat in contrast to that of his father, who was a rather violent man in attitude and action.

When he was twelve, Dan remembers attending another church with a friend. Afterward the minister asked him if he were "saved." To avoid embarrassment, Dan replied that he was. Inwardly he knew he was not, but couldn't bring himself to consider Christ seriously.

After being separated from the service, his father took up work in a sheriff's office in Costa Mesa. But he had little time for his son, and, when he was seventeen, Dan enlisted

OCEAN VIEW CHURCH OF CHRIST
9612 - 26th BAY STREET
NORFOLK, VIRGINIA 23518

in the Naval Reserve. The experience was a horrible one; he rebelled against authority and was sickened by the dishonesty around him. As a result he isolated himself from the others and became a heavy drinker.

After serving his two years he returned to Van Nuys where his parents were then living and enrolled in Valley Junior College. During his college days he was arrested twice for drunken driving. He claims that one night after the first arrest he heard a voice telling him to go to church with his mother and straighten up. He was certain this was the voice of God. He recalls with deep appreciation his mother's helpful attitude through these troubles, but somehow he couldn't or wouldn't respond.

The next year Dan enrolled at Sierra College in Auburn. Here he met Liz and, a short time later, Ted.

Meanwhile, from his second arrest which led to a thirty-day incarceration in jail, he had come away with the idea that dope was better than drink. Hence, if he wished to, Dan could claim the doubtful distinction of being one of the early pot-smoking students of the 1960's.

The Hound of Heaven remained on Dan's trail even in those days. In his search for reality, Dan began to expouse the cause of Communism. This led him later to endorse complete anarchy. A fellow student by the name of Judy became so concerned for him that she invited him to talk with her preacher father who ministered in a neighboring community. Dan accepted Judy's invitation. He remembers the strong emphasis on the destiny of hell for the sinner. And even though he was unwilling to surrender his life to Christ at the pastor's insistence, Dan was not resentful. Even today he says that Judy's friendship and consistency of life were helpful to him then—as well as later—when he was considering the difference between the Christian and the non-Christian life.

Like other emerging hippies of his day, Dan's restlessness soon caught up with him. He decided it was time to move to another school. This time it would be Chico State College and he would major in philosophy.

A week after enrolling he dropped out of school, intent on visiting New York City. He, and a friend, Ed, returned to Auburn to persuade another pal by the name of Mel to join them. When Ted heard of the proposed adventure, he joined the party. The four started out by hitchhiking to Salt Lake City. Then they took a driveaway car to Denver, smoking grass all the way. By the time they arrived, the party had swelled to five fellows and the trip proved to be nothing more than a big "goof off."

When they needed money they worked up a comedy routine and sold the idea to a nightclub. But they soon tired of the monotony of digging up new and dirty jokes and drifted on to other pastures.

Returning home, Dan enrolled in San Jose State College. After a few weeks the academic work became the same old drag. He tossed it aside to participate in an organization called "Acts for Peace." This involved speaking in churches, setting up demonstrations, and promoting nuclear disarmament. The celebrated City Hall Congressional Hearing's riot in San Francisco in May, 1960, jolted him back to reality. Again he was cast adrift emotionally. Desperately he wanted a cause to live for but could find none.

Meanwhile, on the campus of San Jose State, Dan had spotted an attractive, dark-haired girl in a student cooperative called "The Peace Center."

Sandy had spent her childhood in Seattle and Tacoma, Washington. Then her family moved to Cloverdale, California, where she went through high school. She had attended church and Sunday school to some extent, but because her homelife was not particularly happy and the church was meaningless to her parents, she did not continue.

Possessing a good voice, Sandy was given voice lessons during high school and aspired to a professional career. Her parents' lack of interest in her, plus the freedom she had enjoyed from restraints in high school, led to a marriage in her freshman year at San Jose State College. To her dismay Sandy soon learned that her young husband was not interested in a normal married life; he wanted variety. Their move into an apartment in Peace Center proved to be his cup of tea. Sandy grew more and more dissatisfied. Is this all there is to it? she asked herself repeatedly. And when she asked others, no one seemed to know, or at least care.

Then one day Dan appeared at the Peace Center. It didn't take the two long to meet. Dan moved quickly, and they spent a week together.

Sandy knew that this was what she wanted, and asked her husband to leave the apartment. They agreed on a divorce, and Sandy's husband moved in with another girl. When the divorce became final, Dan and Sandy were married on a clergyman's certificate, a provision for couples in common-law marriage.

By now the pattern of Dan's life was well established, and Sandy fitted into it well. They attended classes until they tired of the routine and then went to work. When they wearied of this they took off for Mexico where they remained until their money ran out. Returning broke to San Francisco, they became victims of a wave of Asian flu. Recovering from this, they secured work again and bought a twenty-four-foot sailboat which became their living quarters where it was tied up in the Sausalito harbor.

Here on May 8, 1962, their first daughter, Shannon, was born. Here too Dan reestablished contact with Ted and Liz. When it became apparent that a sailboat was not the best place to rear a creeping baby, their solution was to move to southern California where Dan's mother continued to provide understanding and help. Ted volunteered to help Dan sail the boat down the coast.

Dan went to work painting boats and made good money. They moved into a house by the beach and found the life enjoyable—at least momentarily. It was a carefree, aimless existence, however, and they soon tired of it. The only new dimension they added to their life here was the use of peyote. But its appeal soon paled and they became restless again.

Now they decided to return to San Francisco. Although sailing was Dan's delight, when his prized boat was completely wrecked, the insurance settlement, to Sandi's delight, brought enough cash to buy a truck and a few other desirables to get them back to Sausalito.

First they moved in with Ted and Liz and later found a home for themselves. Back in the center of hippiedom, they quickly reestablished their old ties. Dan moved from one job to another and the family from one house to the next, leaving a trail of unpaid bills behind. Their favorite drug was marijuana, but like their friends they tried them all.

A second daughter, Serafina, was born into this mad scramble on March 9, 1964. Sandy, bright and still very attractive, was able to secure employment easily enough, but she couldn't hold the jobs. Returning to work after Serafina's birth, she followed a routine of turning on with grass in the morning and then going off to work. Both she and Dan became deeply involved with LSD at that time also. But neither was happy with the constant moving, new drugs, fighting and unsettled homelife.

Ted and Dan maintained a close friendship through these years, visiting together at least once a week. After Ted received Christ late in 1965, the visits continued, but the relationship was different. Ted tried to persuade Dan that Christ was the answer to what each had been seeking.

"You've got to believe it, Dan. Jesus is for real," he said.

"Don't give me that stuff, Ted. Look, I've been to church. I've heard what they say. There's nothing to it," Dan replied.

Doggedly Ted persisted.

"Jesus is alive. He's not dead like everybody thinks. You can talk to Him — and He hears you."

"Man, I can't understand how a mover like you can go for this stuff," Dan retorted.

In our midweek prayer meetings Ted would ask for prayer for his friends, especially for Dan. Certainly we didn't know the situations in which these young people lived, but Ted saw to it that we remembered them faithfully in prayer.

Outwardly Dan appeared obdurate. Inwardly a battle was raging. He was watching Ted carefully, eager to find flaws in his friend's new faith in Christ. About this time a severe test came to Ted and Liz when Ted was out of work for an extended period. Skimping to keep the rent paid and groceries on the table, they couldn't afford new tires for their Volkswagen. But Dan knew how to solve that problem. A friend of his used their home as a warehouse for stolen goods. He would have his friend pick up a set of Volkswagen tires for Ted's car. Ted insisted that as a Christian he would not be able to accept them. And when Dan and his friend showed up in Sausalito with the tires, Ted was distressed. When they attempted to put them on his car at the curb, a loud argument erupted. Ted won. Dan was sobered by the sincerity of his friend because he knew Ted's real need for the tires.

At this same time Dan was taking a course on community life at the Free University at Berkeley. There his instructor acknowledged that throughout history only Christian communes had been able to work. And although he didn't subscribe to the Christian faith, he had some awareness of the teaching of the "new birth." When his explanation fell short, another student by the name of Mynra offered, "It's Jesus living in me."

Both the incident and Mynra's description of the Christian life impressed Dan.

On his twenty-eighth birthday, Dan was in deep depres-

55

sion and contemplating either suicide or leaving his family for good. Returning from an outing at Fort Cronkite Beach that day, he and his family stopped to visit Ted and Liz. The warm reception they received convinced Dan that these people who called themselves Christians genuinely cared for them. He had noticed the same feeling on the part of Jim and Judy, who by this time had also acknowledged Christ as their Savior.

Curiously enough, Ted now had begun to wonder how much more time he should spend witnessing to Dan. Then one day he read the biblical warning about being unequally yoked with unbelievers. To him this was a message regarding Dan and Sandy. He told the Lord he would be obedient and stop going to see Dan. However, he would make one more trip in order to explain the reason for the cutoff.

What he didn't know was that Dan had already started to read the Bible to see if he could make it out to be believable. When the two got together, Ted realized for the first time that Dan was actually considering Christ's claim on his life. He pressed him to confess Jesus as his Lord and Savior.

"Say it—just say the words, 'Jesus is my Lord,'" Ted urged.

"I wish I could—but I just can't," said Dan.

The discussion continued for a long time. Ted could think of nothing more to say, so they sat in silence. The seconds stretched into minutes as the clock ticked on.

Dan says that God was bringing his sins into review, and in his mind Dan was asking for forgiveness for them separately. He felt like a drowning man slowly rising to the surface. Suddenly he realized that the whole burden was gone.

"He's done it!" he shouted. "Jesus has forgiven me. He's my Savior and my Lord!"

The experience was a strange and wonderful one for Ted. Having immersed himself in New Testament accounts, he did what naturally came to his mind. He walked over to the chair where Dan was sitting, placed his hands on him, and prayed.

He had scarcely finished when, with a rush of words, Dan began to worship the Lord. Scripture after scripture, which he had no idea he knew, poured from his mouth in a torrent. Both Ted and Dan today believe this was a "prophetic utterance." And I am inclined to agree.

Filled with his new joy and release, Dan rushed into the bedroom where Sandy was asleep. Enthusiastically he described what had happened. "Oh, go to sleep!" was her only response.

But Dan's newfound relationship with Jesus Christ was not to be dimmed by his wife's coolness. And soon she began to see the genuine love that had helped to awaken his response. There *was* a difference, she noted, between her Christian friends and the non-Christians. The final winning witness came when Ted and Liz invited them to move in and share their apartment. Years of restless, turbulent emptiness came to a sudden close for Sandy as she joined her husband within a few days in a united faith in Christ.

And so the scene was now set for the emergence of "The Living Room" and then the "House of Acts"; and those of us at the First Baptist Church of Mill Valley began witnessing the hippie life in our area. Little did any of us know the disturbing, shocking, and exciting events that were to follow

six

What's a Hippie Like?

When I began to prepare Ted for baptism I found him reading the Scriptures with an insatiable hunger, and he talked to all of those around him of what he had found. He did this at work and among his friends. He came to the men's Sunday school class and to the midweek Bible study, entering into every discussion in a way that amazed and rebuked old-timers.

Subjects that could normally be handled with matter-of-fact, calm observations and mild applications, became urgent, demanding issues for Ted. With this new current charging the ecclesiastical atmosphere, nobody was able to fall asleep in our church.

My observations since then have been that one of the characteristics of the hippie community is its desire for spiritual truth. Hence, when a source of spiritual truth such as the Bible is introduced, it is read and discussed freely and openly.

Another common trait among those involved in the hippie life is gregariousness. Since their way of life is in reaction to the institutionalization they have rejected, they find it necessary to establish some sort of code or *modus operandi* by which they live. This often results in involved and sometimes quite meaningless discussion. But transform this native characteristic of gregariousness with the infusion of the Holy Spirit, and the result is dynamic. What was once idle conversation suddenly becomes charged with the power of God, and by traditional Christians it is identified as "witnessing."

To the young Christians in the hippie community, this sort of witnessing is as common in their lives as are money, food and fun for most other social groups. It is a spontaneous activity. No one told Ted to witness. He *had* to tell others what had happened to him. And I truly believe that the same spontaneity has maintained itself with all who come to know Christ through the continuing witness. Before conversion the hippies had lived and suffered within a context of agonizing dialogue. Naturally they pass on the newest thing to their fellows. They don't have to tell new believers to "go out and witness." They have seen their friends doing just that; they have responded to that sort of approach themselves, and hence they know instinctively that this is what they in turn must do.

A third common trait among hippies is that of freely sharing their earthly goods. Before their conversion to Christ, most of those in our hippie community had shared their husbands and wives with others. Their food and drugs were likewise portioned out, so that all who had needs were reasonably supplied.

Now that these flower children had become members of the family of God, this ability to share freely of their earthly goods became a shocking, fearful but also beautiful thing to witness. Once again it appeared to be spontaneous. American youth, dropping out of the so-called Christian society in which they had been reared, have pointed a firm finger of condemnation at the phony Christianity which they see in most of our churches.

Whatever their misunderstanding at times of Christian stewardship and their hasty condemnation of wealthier but earnestly serving Christians, I must concede that my hippie friends have a point. I have been helped, challenged and rebuked—and others of my economic level have had similar experiences—by the manner in which these new converts to Christ have demonstrated their concern for those about them in a physical as well as a spiritual way. Tomorrow doesn't count. If someone needs what one person or family has on hand today, he is freely given what he needs. It's as though the giver knows that the Lord is aware of tomorrow, and that He who provided for today will surely not fail tomorrow. And, just as important is the assumption that our needs are not nearly so great as most of us have come to think. We can get along with much less, and often be happier with it.

The more I have thought about it, the more I am convinced that these three basic traits of the hippie-breed Christian really spell out the love of God which all of us are called upon to emulate. Certainly their zest for knowing the Word of God indicates a wholesome love *for* God. Likewise, their spontaneous sharing of their faith for the people outside of God is a ready response to Christ's Great Commission. And their readiness to share earthly goods is in response to the love for their neighbor which Christ includes in the second part of His first and great commandment. Yet, as admirable—yes, and even disturbing—as I found some of these inherent traits among our young Christian hippies to be, I soon became aware that weaknesses also abounded. Strangely, however, these weaknesses not only evidenced their lack of Christian maturity, but also brought out—in me and other older Christians—characteristics which I was forced to recognize as also something less than full maturity. Out of these times of testing, however, all of us have come to the point of identifying with the witness of Paul: "We are no better than pots of earthenware to contain this treasure, and this proves that such transcendent

61

power does not come from us, but is God's alone" (2 Cor. 4:7, NEB).

Ted's unquenchable thirst for truth showed itself early in his new life. I knew from my first session with him that he was bound to become an active participant in our Bible-exploration studies. How active, I could never have guessed. Questions crowded his conversation. He wasted no time in taking his place in midweek prayer and Bible studies.

But Ted was not simply one to ask questions and be satisfied with any answer. If he didn't understand a statement, he could not drop the matter or wait for a private session. We were made aware of his utter newness in things biblical and, perhaps more to the point, in current evangelical vocabulary. Continually we found it necessary to go back to fundamentals—probing ideas, defining terms, exercising much patience with one another.

Such extended dialogue was interesting to some of the other Bible students present. To others it represented an interruption—even an exasperation.

True, we didn't always cover the points I meant to cover. But we couldn't help but see that here was a man who was hungry to learn. And we had evidence of his willingness to use what he was learning. For prior to our prayer sessions, Ted almost always requested prayer for members of the hippie community in which he lived and moved.

From the beginning, Ted's questions were mixed with opinions. He brought with him, out of his extensive sojourn in psychedelphia, many assumptions about reality. A curt dismissal of some Old Testament passage might be his impulse at the moment. More often it was a dogmatic statement of what a given passage must mean. Very frequently it was a proclamation of pure idealism.

In such Bible study usually one or two individuals are present who converse in idealisms. They project themselves as trusting God, loving others, or being ready to serve.

(What else is there for one who believes the Bible?) Further, if others don't readily agree, they become disturbed.

The presence of such idealists always posed to me the challenge to probe for honesty. Yet I had to admit that Ted had no apparent problem with honesty. His idealism stemmed in part from his old hippie outlook, and in part from the fact that the Bible was new to him. What he read, he accepted at face value and he offered no resistance. This was noticeable to us incrusted believers—especially in Ted's early days.

Most refreshing was his readiness to do whatever he understood God to be requiring of him. Having no buildup of rationalizing Scripture to the point where it could not get a response, he frequently came up with valid insights which the rest of us would miss. And he couldn't understand why others didn't get the message. Continually I found myself pleading with him to be more patient and, at the same time, realistic.

This combination of persistence and sharpness was also capable of rankling other sensitive souls. The sensitivity was often mine.

Moreover, Ted never hesitated to challenge me openly. We would launch into an extended discussion and, at length, break through to common understanding. Typically Ted would conclude with something of a sign.

"Yeah-h-h."

Then I would know we had progressed. But in the meantime, some would come to the conclusion that the sacred had been profaned. And at times I knew Ted was more insistent than he needed to be. Yet I can look back upon those relatively simple experiences and realize that he was only doing what he honestly knew or believed that he had to do.

Another problem of relationship appeared in that formative first year.

We had understood from Ted that his job was in some

jeopardy because his employer was prejudiced against Christianity. Eventually he lost the job because, as he claimed, he refused to be silent about his faith. I must confess I had some reservations about this, since we knew only one side of the story. But we tried to secure work for Ted, and gave his family very limited assistance.

The situation didn't improve when we discovered that Ted was unwilling to take just any job. This kind of attitude does not set well with so-called self-made people. And prospective employers we knew couldn't overlook his even modified hippie appearance.

Much later we learned the other side of the lost-job story. The employer claimed he had exercised much patience, bending over backward to overlook noncooperativeness. Apparently he was not demanding that Ted completely turn off his witness for Christ; rather, he now found the young Christian so aggressively argumentative that his work and that of others were being affected. Hence the termination.

The misunderstanding increased as Liz and Ted found members of our Christian community unwilling to share their material needs. Material abundance displays itself to no small degree in our community, but it was actually their non-Christian hippie friends who were providing for Ted and Liz's sustenance during those difficult times. Sooner or later this disappointment had to surface. And it did—although in an altogether different situation.

Despite their penurious position, Ted and Liz's apartment was crowded with people day and night. Some came for shelter, others to enjoy what food was available, and still others to enjoy the pot they brought along (although Ted and Liz weren't using rugs then, they did not frown on the others doing so). In addition, both Ted and Liz were frequent visitors in the Haight-Ashbury section—moving among old friends and making new acquaintances—with the one purpose of introducing their new Friend, Jesus Christ, to those who so desperately needed Him.

In the process they had found a storefront inhabited by the so-called Diggers, a communal group whose purpose was to provide lodging for those who desperately needed it. They had found a welcome here, and obviously it afforded an unusual opportunity to witness. But now the Diggers' building had been condemned by the health department and the whole operation was on the point of folding up. In his own calm but definite way, Ted put the question to me.

"I want to know," he announced, "is the church willing to help in a time of need like this? I want to show these Diggers that church people do care about them....So can we offer them the use of our church building?"

Behind a defensive shield of what must have been a pitiful stammer, my mind was trying to put together quickly all the pieces of a complex picture. To say yes was out of the question. Even though I could foresee difficulties, it was not my prerogative to speak on behalf of the board of deacons. But to say no bluntly could also turn away forever from the organized church what appeared to me to be a growing opportunity to meet the spiritual need of a group of young people.

What could I say or do? Cautiously I began to spell out the difficulties:

"Even if the church is willing, probably our insurance would not permit this kind of use of the building—and insurance coverage *is* a legal necessity. And, of course, since we are across the Golden Gate in Marin County, what real help will this be for Haight-Ashbury?" I temporized.

seven

The Living Room Is Born

"All I want," persisted Ted, "is to be able to make this gesture. It's important to us to be able to make this offer of friendship for the church."

He was talking, of course, about his idea of offering our chuch as a pad for a group of hippies.

"I can go along with that," I said, "but the practical and honest truth of the matter is that we could not allow these hippie people to stay in our church. It would violate the building code."

"Man, why do we always have to get hung up over laws when there are human needs?" Ted replied. His hostility to the Establishment was now showing. "We find out pretty quickly who our real friends are," he said grimly.

His voice remained soft, but his words were hard. I was sure he was being hopelessly unrealistic, but I was fearful he would give up on us. My hope was to keep him in a place where we could really help him, so I opened up.

"Ted, I happen to know you've just paid a license fee to the state of California so that you can continue to drive your car. Why did you give in to the Establishment at this point? How far do you think any church would get if it defied the laws? You're not going to help anybody with this kind of intimidation."

In my anger I punched away. Ted hung on.

"I've been honest with you about using the church building, but I'm willing to go into the city with you and look over the situation. If there is anything within law and reason we can do, I'd like to know," I finally said. I concluded with a promise to call agencies and churches of that area to see what could be done about the Diggers' problem.

That afternoon a tour of Haight-Ashbury was taken by two men with mutual respect, sincere concern, and ability to communicate. I was learning that this man who didn't hesitate to dish out a rough challenge could also take the same in return. But I've also learned to observe that when people don't understand these personal dynamics, they quickly get turned off by Ted and his friends.

One more incident which occurred about this time further illustrates how far apart we were in our understanding of one another.

I was to be away from the church for our midweek prayer service. In order to keep my agreement with Ted to find help for the Diggers, I suggested to Ted that he give his testimony that evening at prayer meeting—something he had not yet done fully in our church. This, I thought, might indicate how interested our people would be in witnessing to the hippie community.

But, instead of giving his testimony, Ted brought in a group of hippie friends together with a collection of recordings of their typical music. His idea was to show by means of the lyrics how very deep and sincere is the hippie philosophy, and to point out how beautifully the gospel can meet this plaintive search. Regrettably, the music was too much for many of those present. To this day I am sure some haven't yet recovered.

Clearly, the tactical error was mine. I should have been present to control the meeting, but this illustrates how slow I was in learning. But if I thought this was all there was to it, I was sadly mistaken. For I still had much more to learn — as the events of the next few months were to show.

How could we ever help young people who chose the hippie way of life? Ted, a hippie convert, had said we weren't interested. How could I prove to him that he was wrong?

As a result of the encounter with Ted over how to help the Diggers, I took my first serious tour of Haight-Ashbury.

Ted and I strolled the streets and entered several establishments together. I noted the ease with which he related to the citizens there — and the estrangement with respect to myself. By dress and appearance, he belonged. Clearly I did not. He readily stopped for a few words or to give some money to someone in need. Obviously he had remarkable rapport.

Gradually an idea began to emerge. This was an unexplored field of evangelism. It was crawling with young people in all of their familiar trappings: long hair, beards and beads. Official projections expected the summer population for that particular year to explode at more than 100,000 hippies moving in and out of Haight-Ashbury. We sat and talked outside the Diggers' condemned headquarters.

"God has been talking to Liz and me," said Ted. "I believe He wants us to spend our full time here witnessing to these kids — and we're ready to do it."

I didn't dare ask him, "But how will you support yourself and family?" I knew his answer would probably be, "Well, isn't this the responsibility of the Christian community?" And inwardly, I knew he was perfectly right.

Yet, at the same time Ted was too far from what I considered to be a mature believer with a balanced understanding of Scripture and an appreciation of what was meant by Christian living to become a full-fledged missionary. Not that there wasn't sufficient money around for such a good cause. But who was ready to contribute to the work for hippies and especially to put his money in the hands of an outspoken rebel like Ted? So I hedged.

"This might be a very good idea," I said.

But, for all of my halting realism, I was captivated. God seemed to be saying to me, "Here is a breakthrough that is tailored for Haight-Ashbury. As you know, you didn't take any initiative here, nor did you have any idea of what could be done for hippies until Ted came along. I've provided all of this—you must trust Me for the rest." So, before we left the scene that afternoon, Ted and I prayed together in my parked car, and I came home determined to let God open the way.

But whatever hope I had cherished that our church might respond was soon shattered. Ted managed to offend a number of our church members, primarily in an effort to explain the hippie scene over which he had presided at the prayer meeting. Thus, to my mind, it became clear that there was no way to persuade an existing church, or group of churches, or even a Christian agency, to undertake support for believing hippies for a Haight-Ashbury mission —at least without exasperating delays.

However, God was not without His encouragement. It soon appeared that there were men at hand who could read the facts without being slowed down by prejudice or personal offense. The result was a new and independent organization and called Evangelical Concerns, Inc. Those who responded to the idea included Dr. John Streater, pastor of San Francisco's First Baptist Church, and his assistant, Dr. Howard Day; the Rev. Edward Plowman of Park Presidio Baptist Church in San Francisco, and the Rev. William Mansdoerfer, executive director of Family Radio, a chain of FM stations with headquarters in San Francisco. Others who attended our first meeting included George Hardisty, local attorney; the Rev. Jack Karman, veteran rescue-mission operator; and O. Eugene Pitts, director of Christian education at the First Baptist Church of San Francisco.

Ted had already come up with the idea of a person-to-person approach rather than a typical rescue-mission program. His plan was to open a center for relaxed conversation and he had even worked out the name, "The Living Room."

In fact, Ted was already at work, so he didn't switch suddenly from one kind of occupation to another. Haight-Ashbury was there, and he knew his way around. Even without a definite address, his contacts expanded every day.

Our intent, so far as financial support was concerned, was to appeal to Christians of the area. We knew it would take some time before funds would be sufficient to pay our one missionary a living wage, so we suggested that Ted continue at his sailmaking trade until adequate funds would be coming in to support him and his family.

But Ted soon became so overwhelmed by the potentials of his new mission field that he quit his job altogether in order to devote more time to witnessing. Helpers rushed to his aid—Steve and Sandi, Jim and Judy, Dan and Sandy, young converts. Meanwhile, Ted and Liz's apartment in Sausalito was overrun with hippie life.

In late summer of 1967 the Living Room was opened in a storefront in the Armenian Hall on Page Street, one block from Haight Street and close to the center of the hippie scene—and also to Golden Gate Park panhandle, where hippie "be-ins" were breaking out spontaneously.

Immediately the place became crowded with youngsters —lonely, hungry, and, above all, caught in frightening circumstances and needing assurance of friendship rather than the exploitation which too often was their lot.

Many of them plaintively acknowledged that the hippie scene was not so glamorous after all. Their plea was for help. Others came while high on acid or other drugs and needing support from someone who understood the experience. Some claimed to know Jesus Christ but continued to live in the scene of dope addiction and fornication. Many others acknowledged Jesus Christ as Lord but had no perception at all of Him as the Son of God who was crucified to save them from their sins.

Obviously the devil wouldn't let a situation as productive as this develop without an attack. And attack he did—again at the core of our relationship with one another and our understanding of the meaning of the Word of God.

eight

Trouble Brews

During vacation Bible school that summer two of our former hippie wives were helping. At the same time, I was preparing a series of Sunday morning sermons on Christian citizenship.

To my surprise one weekday morning, one of the girls asked, "Why in the world do you have the children salute the American flag in church?"

She was genuinely perplexed, and I was momentarily speechless.

"Well, I'm going to be preaching on that subject Sunday morning," I mumbled. "I'm sure you'll find it helpful."

Sunday morning saw the full group in their places two or three pews deep. I preached on the theme, "Is Patriotism Christian?" with my text from 1 Peter 2:1-17. Response was good, and there were no visible problems. The next Sunday three hippies responded to the invitation. Their intent, they said, was to make a public declaration of faith in Christ but not to be baptized or join the church. This was an understandable position for them to take, and I assumed that in

73

given time they would also accept baptism and membership. (I had just baptized Dan and Sandy.)

The following Sunday my preaching brought me to the subject, "Criminals and Christians." It was a presentation of God's purposes in ordaining civil rulers, with an emphasis on the limitations of civil rule, and the power of the gospel to effect real change in people's lives. I dealt directly with the issues of capital punishment, and was reaching the climax of my appeal for the gospel witness when the unexpected occurred. The man who had come forward the week before, stood up and faced me.

"Brother, you make me sick!" he said and stalked out.

I managed to compose myself and finish the message.

After church I expressed my regret for his action to Dan.

"I don't mind the fact that he disagreed with me, but that sort of reaction doesn't help any of us," I said.

"I suppose so," Dan agreed mildly.

But, as developments later proved, none of the group at that time agreed with me wholeheartedly. To them, the Bible could not possibly require anything but pacifism and a no-death standard. Augustine's "just war" concept was obviously false, so don't bother to mention it.

Group insurrection came the following Sunday.

This time my sermon extended the subject of civil rule and Christian responsibility. Outside church afterward I approached one of the women to compliment her on her musical presentation. She had something else in mind, and now became the group's spokesman.

"We don't like the liberal, unbiblical sermons you've been preaching," she asserted.

"I guess I don't understand what you mean," I said, surprised.

The argument which followed was not easy, but I stood my ground. When God said that civil rulers were His appointed servants, I insisted, He meant just that. But these new citizens of heaven retorted that being "subject to the powers that be" meant to *submit if necessary*, but certainly *never to support*. The structures of this world, they said, are hopelessly corrupt and have nothing to offer the Christian. They would never vote or do anything to support civil government, they insisted.

This attitude toward restrictions soon cropped up on other fronts.

Ted and Liz had continually made room for visitors in their little apartment in Sausalito. Regardless of how crowded it was, there was always room for one more. This, they felt, was their Christian duty.

And when their landlord said that either they must put out their friends or get out altogether, their response was simple: "Should we listen to God or to him?" The obvious implications were that it was from God—not men—that they were getting their signals. In other words, when someone needs help, you help. Regulations are forgotten under these circumstances. In this case, however, the landlord was not so understanding; they were evicted.

The same problem appeared in connection with the "Living Room." Our rental agreement provided that no one was to sleep there overnight. But if someone came along who had no other place to sleep, quite naturally he was invited to spend the night there.

It was not long, of course, before the landlord discovered the violation and came to us.

It seemed obvious to the members of the board of directors of Evangelical Concerns that our young hippie Christians needed some biblical indoctrination. As chairman, I was given the responsibility. A time was set when I would meet with the staff of the Living Room for Bible study.

On the Wednesday evening preceding the first class, three of the staff and one or two others came to our church prayer meeting. It was November 1, the day after the 450th anniversary of Luther's nailing his Ninety-five Theses to the church door. On that significant occasion I was prepared to introduce a study of Luther's theses. I was glad for the presence of our converted hippies because this would be a good introduction to the study of doctrine they were about to begin. As an opening, I planned to read an article by a well-known evangelical theologian, and then use it as a take-off point.

At least, so I thought.

I began by reading a few of the theses and then turned to the article by the modern-day theologian. A distinct rumble came from the hippie Christians. Hurriedly—and quite confidently also—I began to explain the value of church history and the fact that today's church offers many elements contrary to God's Word.

Then Ted stood up. Turning to the book of Galatians, he read the opening lines of Paul's letter.

"Paul made his position clear from the beginning," he said. "And this man you are quoting in the article, we don't know where he stands."

Before I could make clear why I had introduced the article, another hippie convert spoke out.

"We have no business reading anything but the Bible. Everything else is human opinion and a waste of time."

I was dumbfounded. "If that is true," I asked, "how can we even talk and listen to one another?"

"Oh, conversation is fine," they replied. "It's just printed matter that's wrong. There is something too unreal about someone's words in print."

By this time the group assault was taking shape, and I was unable to hold a single line of thought or to return to my subject. My disagreement was turning to outrage. During recent weeks I had had the uneasy feeling that my future contacts with this group might be limited. Now, before our church members and leaders, an actual rupture was taking place.

But they have chosen to disrupt what I'm doing as a minister of the gospel, I reasoned. *And I can't meekly assent to that.*

76

I assured them of my own great appreciation for the numerous writings in my library and elsewhere and that this was sheer presumption on their part. Further, I said that I recognized their right to be immature as young Christians —still actually "babes in Christ." Hence, I told them they should be willing to listen to others who had gone on ahead of them.

But I was getting nowhere. And since Ted was the leader in the fray, I finally addressed him with a voice that broke with emotion.

"Ted, I am very disturbed and very sorry to see you come to this. What you're doing isn't Christlike."

Then I dismissed the meeting.

In the aftermath of the meeting I was told by Ted and the others that they were doing what they had to do.

"The Holy Spirit directed us," they said.

I retorted promptly. "I sensed the presence of a spirit —but not the Holy Spirit."

Ted smiled with confidence. "Then where did the Holy Spirit go?"

I assured him that he was indeed subject to temptation, and I hoped he would at least consider the possibility that he had been wrong in what he had done. But Ted could see no reason why the actions he and the others had taken were sinful.

Heavyhearted, the next day I joined John Streater, Howard Day and Eugene Pitts at the First Baptist Church in San Francisco. I related the events of the previous evening.

"Seems to me, John, I have sensed a growing sharpness between you and Ted," John Streater observed.

"I suppose you're right," I admitted. "But Ted is direct, and I've found that he responds best to direct replies, and I'll admit that they're foreign to my nature."

"And as a result you don't carry them off too well," Streater said.

I felt badly. But we prayed together and my sorrow

77

appeared to lift some. In the days that followed I asked interested friends to pray also.

But the more I thought about it, there no longer seemed to be any good reason for beginning a study of Bible doctrine with the staff at the House of Acts. I wasn't about to make myself an object of abuse and give them another invitation to censure the Establishment. I simply didn't go.

When the second meeting night rolled around, I didn't go again. Then the telephone rang; it was Ted.

"Sorry you couldn't make the meeting last week. We waited an hour for you, and we're waiting now."

I reminded him of what happened the week before in church, and repeated my feelings that they weren't really looking for help.

Ted's voice and words were those of a man with strong confidence. He was in the driver's seat and began to open up. He reminded me of the first year of his contacts with our church, and of our caution in coming to the help of new Christians.

"I've had my belly full of the established church. I don't want anything more to do with it," he said evenly.

As before, we got nowhere with one another, and I could see no point in continuing the conversation. But Ted seemed intent upon making me listen.

Finally I spoke up. "I recognize your gifts, but I also recognize that you are a long way short of where you think you are. I am not going to continue this hopeless argument."

Then I hung up.

When Marilyn came in I reported that I had just likely concluded our association with Ted and company. My wife and I were a sad pair.

Within an hour there was a step outside and the doorbell rang. When I opened it, Ted and Jim walked in.

"Well," I blurted, "I guess I'm not really surprised to see you."

Jim explained that since he hadn't been present at the

prayer meeting blowup he really didn't know what all the problem was about. "But we're brothers in Christ," he said. "Seems to me we ought to be able to come to some Christian agreement."

Maybe this was the first time something became clear to me; I am not sure. At least that evening I saw a characteristic in Ted and the others which I had never noted before. No matter what disagreements arose, they didn't take anything as personally offensive. Tonight they were not about to give up on me.

Gradually we were able to warm up to one another, with a growing sense of belonging to a fellowship of believers. Gradually, too, we began to consider the fact of temptation. This proved to be a turnabout in their thinking. Illustrations from the Bible were discussed, and I ventured to offer Ted the words Jesus spoke to Peter just before his betrayal: "Simon, Simon, take heed: Satan has been given leave to sift all of you like wheat; but for you I have prayed that your faith may not fail; and when you have come to yourself, you must lend strength to your brothers" (Lk. 22:31-32, NEB).

Ted thought he had an answer for this too in the change brought about in Peter at Pentecost. But then we discussed Peter's later faults, as well as Paul's. And soon we found an honest kind of sinful kinship with the apostles and other great servants of Christ. After this it was easy for us to conclude with a humble prayer. And as the men went out that night, Ted embraced me warmly.

This incident didn't stop Ted's challenges to me. But I knew a different relationship existed between us.

I did return to the Living Room and we began our study of the book of Romans on a weekly basis. Almost immediately a new growth emerged for all of us. I definitely include myself.

Did this mean our troubles were over? Hardly.

As soundly converted as an increasing number of these

hippie men and women were, they were nonetheless still "converted hippies." Many of the men still wore their hair long and supported full beards. Both men and women went barefooted. And pot was still smoked by some, while others still dropped acid.

Clearly more trouble lay ahead.

nine

Battle over Drugs

Marijuana—or pot, grass, or mary jane, as it is also called—is a basic drug on the hippie scene. Its use was almost universal wherever so-called hippies were and are found. And today it is entering the acceptable social scene as a substitute for alcoholic beverages. Recent studies reveal that in New York City twelve out of fifteen industries indicated that drug use (specifically marijuana) is becoming an increasing problem with both blue-and white-collar workers.

In our early days of contact with hippies, this hallucinogen had reached an illicit traffic of frightening proportions. In fact, the use of pot had become so common that we discovered it took some time before a convert could recognize the danger its use could be to his Christian life and testimony.

Hence, our consistent policy was to help the hippie acknowledge Jesus Christ as his Lord and Savior, and then, through prayer and Bible study, to show him how the Holy Spirit could help him recognize sins and then gain victory over them.

Almost all of the men and women in our group had been

habitual pot smokers. I watched their struggle with considerable interest and sympathy. From the beginning of our experience with Ted, I determined to let him learn and decide for himself what to do about it—and so also with the others. Laying down rules of conduct, outside of those specified in the Word of God, is not my understanding of the best means to sponsor Christian maturity. It certainly was not indicated so far as the thinking hippie was concerned.

At several points I picked up remarks by members of the group that they either wanted to quit or were actually in the process of quitting. Meanwhile, others who had stopped smoking were urging them to do so. On several occasions I observed that all of them had simultaneously kicked the habit. But, subsequently I would note that the practice had come back—first by a few and then by almost everyone. I had the strong feeling when the waves of smoke came on that I was not giving the prayer support I should.

One factor was that some had had a much harder time than others in kicking the habit. And once they returned, the others were soon infected. Their very communal life added to the problem. Again, the House of Acts and the Living Room were always open to all comers, and no one was prohibited from smoking. Even with the staff and wives abstaining, the problem continued to be great.

Sad to say, even Christians have accused our group of using and promoting the use of marijuana. This may have come from the naive way in which our staff and other young converts exchange information freely and often were misunderstood by straight Christians.

Also, we had received some publicity. First came an article in the local press, then a full-length feature in *Christian Life* magazine and later one in *Christianity Today* and another in *Baptist Leader*. While information of this sort was helpful in getting the interest and prayer support of earnest Christians, at the same time it attracted others who were eager to criticize.

One of the most difficult incidents came through contact with a nationally known and respected Christian leader. He called members of our staff and arranged for pictures and taped interviews. But in the midst of what started on a warm, friendly note, our men found themselves being manipulated. Crucial questions revolved about their attitude toward marijuana and, in spite of mild protests, our men were made to look as though they were indifferent to pot and even promoting its use.

The taped encounter was soon run on local television, appearing even more damaging in its edited version. Next the film made the rounds of the country, the leader using it to demonstrate the superiority of his evangelistic approach over that of our hippie believers.

There were indeed some differences in policy toward drug use. As mentioned earlier, our concern has been to get the individual to first acknowledge the good news of forgiveness of sins through faith in Christ—then to bring his faith to bear on the problem of drugs. We had been led to this approach because hippies are intellectually active and peacefully inclined. On the other hand, those non-Christians with whom our antagonists worked, came from a much different background, intellectually as well as socially.

Of course we believe that the use of drugs is a false way to God or life. Drugs do not lead to true faith in God nor are they compatible with Christian faith. They are similar to many other practices with which the young believer must contend.

In each case, as attacks such as this and others were made, members of our board of directors carefully questioned Ted and his co-workers. Uniformally they denied the charges, and I issued official denials of pot-smoking Bible-study sessions and the use of any hallucinogens or narcotics by our staff. Thus we were able to blunt some of the criticism that could have been most damaging to all of us.

But we were not without error. True enough, the charges were usually exaggerated and thus easily refuted. Regrettably, I learned much later that there was some substance to the criticism. And the time came when our group faced up to its own failures with real heart-searching. For in the Bible-study sessions, the meaning of "stumbling blocks," as Paul discusses Christian responsibility for others in Romans 14, deeply affected some individuals.

For example, Dan had some months earlier faced the issue for himself, and had become fully committed to forsaking pot altogether. Others, however, had been permitting themselves occasional lapses, as visitors would come into the Living Room smoking. Then a number of the young believers shared a deep spiritual experience and, as a result, agreed to give up marijuana forever. This, I believe, was our last major struggle over drugs.

Other problems of misunderstanding also cropped up.

One of these involved the so-called "hippie appearance." Even after conversion, our young believers continued to rebel against established customs of dress, hair arrangements, social mores, etc. They stoutly denied that they were rebelling against Jesus Christ.

To many Christians of the Establishment, however, this represented a serious issue. On my part, I had to honestly ask myself the question, "Who established the current styles?"

In the end, I must admit it was those of us of the Establishment who made the concessions. "Outward appearances," we agreed, "didn't determine a man's devotion to Christ."

Another situation which our straight Christian community did not understand—probably because they did not appreciate it—was the communal life in which our hippie Christians were involved. As I mentioned earlier, because Ted and Liz's apartment was continuously overcrowded, their landlord gave them an eviction notice. On one of my visits to the apartment shortly afterward, I was greeted by this happy announcement.

"We're going to compose a Christian community, having all things in common just like the early Christians."

Of course, only a realistic old Christian such as I would raise the question, "How did the sharing efforts in the book of Acts work out?"

Nobody appeared to even hear what I was saying. At least, none of that deliriously happy troupe appeared to question the rightness of the episode in the book of Acts or the idea that had for a "House of Acts" to house the basic family group of seventeen people, children and adults, and the ebb and flow of other hippies to whom they witnessed day after day.

As I reflected further on what was happening, and on their singleness of mind as to the Christian communal project, I was persuaded to hold my peace.

Perhaps, I thought, *these later-day converts are actually retracing the steps of the early church more than other Christians of my acquaintance. If the first Christians were given freedom by the Holy Spirit to test their ideas against the realities of human nature, why shouldn't these young people have the same experience?*

Clearly, their joy and confidence appeared to have no bounds, and their actions really did remind us of that early church life described by Luke. By summer's end the right place was found. A substantial and spacious old ranch house was rented in Novato, a suburb twenty miles south of Sausalito. I regretted seeing them move so far away, especially since it would mean they could no longer be active in our church. But I was confident God had His own plans.

Jack Shaw, a veteran sea captain and himself a recent convert to Christ, came up with the name, "House of Acts," and one of the first Christian hippie communes, if not *the* first, was born on the West Coast.

I was fascinated to watch the communal life emerge.

One of the first problems was discipline. This began with the children. Prior to merging their life-styles, each family had its own approach — or lack of it.

In joining forces, they agreed to one system. In effect,

every adult became a parent to every child. This meant that each adult opened his heart in acceptance and love as well as in correction for each child.

Probably the most significant aspect of this development was the emergence of a clear understanding of original sin. In becoming Christians, these adults had difficulty at this point. Now as they saw this sinful nature arising in their children, they were forced to face it responsibly. In fact, Ted once said in my hearing that not until they had accepted the responsibility of communal living had he and Liz learned to punish children for their disobedience.

More tricky, but equally interesting, was the emergence of "authority" in the adult community.

ten

Life in a Commune

The four men who emerged as leaders in the new Christian commune continually worked for harmonious solutions or decisions. No one ever claimed to be the head man. Ted, although by seniority able to presume leadership, continually disclaimed it. In fact, at times it appeared that Jim was the spokesman.

Other individual roles became clarified in time. Dan was the soft-spoken peacemaker. Steve was the intelligent, articulate public relations man. But all worked together in an amazing kind of teamwork.

Although I never witnessed the men crossing family lines to lay down the law to the women, there was a strong assumption of authority by the male contingent. The community was in agreement that this was the biblical way. On a few occasions I felt that this authority was too strongly exercised, for the Bible does require a man to be gentle and not to humiliate his wife before others. Yet the women continually displayed willing submission to their husbands and appeared quite secure in their new order of life.

It also appeared to me on some occasions that the men were not always aware of the need of their wives for rest. While the men were away on evangelistic activities, the women bore a large share of the communal burden. For a full year no one of the commune held full-time remunerative employment. All of the men felt that their obedience to God meant full-time involvement with hippie and youth evangelism. They willingly accepted brief stints at housepainting or sailmaking in order to keep rent and grocery money coming in. Ted alone was "on salary" with Evangelical Concerns, but this was purely a matter of how much money came in over and above what was needed to keep the Living Room open.

This meant the women had their work cut out for them. Hippie training came to their aid. Some knew well enough how to glean from the grocers, and their good manners and attitudes resulted in sympathetic cooperation. Once the local grocers had identified them as worthy people, they were permitted access to the throw away produce and other perishable items.

On one of my frequent visits to the House of Acts, Steve identified the dish as "rice grotesque," since it was the second or third day's appearance. All enjoyed the humorous reference, and no one complained. So far as I am aware, no meals were missed. Clearly, however, this was in large part due to their willingness to meet their Provider halfway. And they never failed to acknowledge that the source of every gift was God—or to open their table to visitors, of which there were often many.

The hardworking wives applied their gifts tirelessly. Some cooked well, others preferred clean-up chores. Some sewed cleverly. Others did gardening. Every day that the men went into Haight-Ashbury and the Living Room, they took a large pot of vegetable soup that was cooked the night before. That soup kettle was an institution in itself and never seemed to leave the stove.

88

What impressed me above everything else is that these young Christian men and women were willing to pay the price to do what they believed God wanted them to do. They were content with a simple life: joy in the Lord is what it was.

And of all the notable characteristics evidenced in the House of Acts, I would have to place Christian fellowship as the most impressive. Frequently arriving for Bible study while the expanded family was at the dinner table, Marilyn and I watched the community engaged in this kind of fellowship.

Among adults, there seemed to be no end of serious biblical discussion. They were doing what they wanted to do, and God's Word was opening to them as a wonderful, exciting force. Nothing else appeared nearly so important. Each one was studying regularly and was able to participate. All listened to what each had to offer. Commonly they responded with gratitude and spontaneity.

"Oh, yeah, that's right—I hadn't thought of it that way."

Even disagreements were handled with courtesy and consideration for everyone.

The openness of the House of Acts to all comers was practically without limit. Sleeping bags and their occupants often covered floors and even extended to the porch. Many a true hippie with exterior trappings, oriental religious jargon, drugs and other forms of "freedom" in full evidence, was given the genuine warmth of Christian hospitality. And always an unashamed witness for Christ was evidenced. The excited exclamations of victory often followed.

One of the most rewarding developments, to me at least, was the response of local youth to the witness of the House of Acts. Attracted by the colorfully dressed personnel at the House of Acts, local high school young people were quick to drop in and see what it was all about. As they were caught up in the conversation and stayed for the Bible studies, it was natural that many of them also submitted their lives to Jesus Christ. Naturally the local police followed with their own investigation. Subsequently, they became appreciative friends who themselves found the House of Acts a friendly place to visit.

Looking back now, it appears to me that the core of our early difficulties in understanding one another lay in the mystical approach of the hippie to life in general.

The true non-Christian hippie is not simply a beatnik bent on having a high time with drugs, fornication and loafing. Primarily he is a youth who has judged our culture as barren, hypocritical, unloving and materialistic. His impulse is to "drop out" of this "decadent society," and to get "turned on" in a life of love and simplicity.

Obviously he has not come up with a serious philosophy that faces the real problems of life, and so he has no valid answers. He is pitifully naive in his expectation of a beautiful life of love. As a result, he easily becomes the sad victim of drug addiction, venereal disease and a hopeless futility.

Today this "pure hippie" philosophy—indeed, even the whole hippie way of life—may be passing as a trend in the night. But the concern of young people today for the reality of a mystical experience has not passed. Nor do I believe it will for a long time. The materialistic world which our generation has cultivated has proved a fraud. It promised the good life but, in their opinion has failed completely to provide anything but war, privation, pollution, and civil corruption.

With this background, the new Christian born out of the mystical hippie scene develops what I call the "overconfidence syndrome." Since he is already convinced that the Establishment, including the church, is dead, he is not overawed by human authority. Thus he readily and openly pits his "revelations" against any authority. Of course, this is where he runs into most of his problems within the church. Whether or not the average church today is secure enough to allow him to grow into the necessary maturity is another question.

Long ago I learned that this type of young person will resist more than anything else the efforts of people like me to reduce or undercut his mysticism. He does not easily see that his direct "revelations" may conflict with the revelations of other mystics. Moreover, when these people accept Christ as their personal Savior and Lord, they have usually done so on the basis of what they have read from the Word of God. Hence, they don't want me to tell them that this is God's *whole* special revelation. When I stress this I am criticized for being proud and for denying the power of God.

I must admit frankly that God has taught me much through these experiences. And I am aware that my hippie friends are often dismayed that I cannot enjoy the fullness of the faith that is theirs. At the same time I have been encouraged greatly as I have seen the Spirit of God teach them more effectively than I could have possibly done. Plainly, all those who read the Bible as consistently, pray as regularly, and witness to their faith as eagerly as these people do, will be led into the truth of God. Of this I am confident.

So it is little wonder that as we emerged from many of the troublesome areas, evidence of the power of God at work in the Living Room and in the House of Acts burgeoned. Almost every week I witnessed to or heard of new conversions to Christ, deliverances from LSD, or answers to prayer for everything from physical healing to necessary shoes and clothing for the children. For I could not be completely honest unless I also gave testimony to the fact that God did move indeed in a supernatural way. And while some of my theological friends might demur at the suggestion that the gifts of the Holy Spirit as evidenced in the record of the early church could be operational today, yet both my Christian hippie friends and I could produce evidence that would be hard to refute.

These were exciting days. And it seemed as if the tempo increased daily.

eleven

Witness of the House of Acts

The incredible stories of some of the young people who found their way to the fellowship of the Living Room or the House of Acts come as astonishing demonstrations of the power of the Holy Spirit to transform lives.

A dramatic illustration is Marc, born into a conservative Jewish home in Brooklyn, New York, on October 25, 1938. As an intelligent and eager junior high school youth, Marc read the New Testament and recognized its claim to be the fulfillment of the Old Testament prophecies. But because he knew of no one who lived up to the New Testament standards, he concluded that the account was simply a fanciful tale.

Although his family did not practice Jewish ritual, they were committed to its social and ethical standards. Hence, by the time Marc's father died at the close of the youth's high school career, he had received good home training, had been taught not to be gullible, and yet, open to reason. He read widely, and although he did not attend college, he circulated with friends in the orbit of New York University. Here he came under the influence of Bertrand Russell's humanism. His peace with God, he decided, could be made later.

Then Timothy Leary and his LSD gospel loomed on the scene. Marc met Leary and talked with him on several occasions. He experimented with the drug and came to believe it was a gift of God to mankind.

At twenty-two, Marc was married, and a year and a half later divorced. A daughter born of the marriage remained with Marc until she was five. Then, realizing how much emotional damage she was suffering from the lack of a proper homelife, Marc endured the painful experience of giving her up for adoption.

Meanwhile, beacuse he was convinced that LSD was a boon to humanity, Marc had established connections with a chemist who was producing LSD. Over a period of eleven years he claims to have given away more than seventeen million doses without charge. In addition, he acted as chief distributor for the manufacturer, working only thirty to sixty days each year. His profits kept him in a plush apartment in Manhattan while he attended the Met, the Ballet, and the best of theatrical fare. At the same time he held down a strictly blue-collar job as a Railway Express employee.

On one of his "business trips to pick up some LSD in Denver, Marc left New York City with $7,000 in his pocket. Somewhere along the way his pocket was picked and he landed in Denver with only enough money for one meal. In the restaurant he saw a poster advertising IXOYE House. These Greek letters spell *Ichthys* a Greek word meaning "fish." It is one of the oldest Christian symbols. Ancient Christians used the sign of the fish secretly since its letters stood for "Jesus Christ, God's Son, Savior." Although Marc did not understand this, he did understand the additional line on the poster which said, "Crashers welcomed."

At the IXOYE House Marc found hostess Diane and host

Mickey, two charming young people who lived up to the standards of the New Testament. He decided that this was what he wanted also, and so, without hesitation, opened his heart to Jesus Christ.

Curiously enough, Diane and Mickey had been converted to Christ through the ministry of the Living Room and the House of Acts back in the San Francisco area. They had opened the IXOYE House in Denver to minister the gospel of Christ to the hippies passing through the city. Properly sleeping in separate rooms, they now decided that God wanted them to minister as husband and wife. Knowing the friendly hospitality of their former habitat, they determined to return to the fellowship of the House of Acts to be united in marriage.

Marc followed several days later in order to witness the ceremony and enjoy the Christian fellowship he had learned about from Diane and Mickey. Here he came under conviction of his use of LSD and kicked the habit. At the Living Room he saw a sign inviting him to attend the First Baptist Sunday school picnic at Golden Gate Park. Despite his hippie attire, he was warmly welcomed. The next day he attended church and found the same acceptance. This, he decided, was where he belonged. Later he submitted to church requirements, was baptized by the Rev. John Streater, and became a member of the church. And amazingly, several days later he was named by the church to serve as a delegate to the Baptist state convention at San Jose in 1968.

A marriage which took place a few months later involved young people named Connie and Lonnie, both of whom were rescued from the depths of human despair by the witness of members of the Christian hippie community.

Connie had been in and out of juvenile halls and foster homes as long as she could remember. She graduated from this to a string of free-living relationships, during which time she lost or quit a variety of jobs.

She had begun to drink early and this soon gave way to the use of drugs. Her drug habit meant that she had to steal. For this, as well as drug possession, she had been busted on a number of occasions. While living in one commune in Southern California, Connie met Lonnie.

In his earlier years Lonnie had had some sort of spiritual experience. But there had been little interest in him at home; he had rebelled and left.

The two young people met and were attracted to one another. In his search for reality, Lonnie had picked up a gospel of John somewhere. This he read to himself and aloud to Connie who became interested in trying to find God.

But, being of a restless nature, she soon left the commune at Silverado Canyon to visit others at Mount Shasta, Big Sur and elsewhere. Although continually stoned on acid, portions of Scripture that Lonnie had read to her kept coming into her troubled mind.

Meanwhile, Lonnie had made contact with the Living Room and, although not yet clear as to its full meaning, he had made a commitment of his life to Jesus Christ. One day he started hitchhiking to Los Angeles, but because of poor rides, he turned back. On the way back to his surprise and delight, he met Connie, to whom he fervently witnessed about Christ. Even though he still held confused ideas, and she was stoned on acid, she began to understand the gospel of Christ for the first time. Connie acknowledged Jesus as her personal Savior and Lord, and they stopped at Tahquitz Falls where Lonnie baptized her.

Spontaneous baptism, incidentally, while certainly not approved by most organized churches, not by all straight members of evangelical concerns, is a fairly common part of the converted-hippie scene. Despite my counsel, they have read about the evangelist Phillip and the Ethiopian eunuch and have not yet been impressed by arguments urging caution and official church action.

96

Shortly after Connie's capitulation, Lonnie took her to the House of Acts. Here they both lived, benefiting from the steadier example and counsel of the older house members, from the enriching Bible study, and the opportunity of a co-operative witness for Christ. After six months, their wedding took place.

The ceremony made quite a splash on the local scene. It was solemnized in a Novato Lutheran Church and rated an extensive society-column write-up and picture in the local press. Youths and adults from both here and Marin County attended. The mixture of traditional ceremony with the couple's artistic innovations created quite a stir, since both bride and groom wore garlands of daisies in their hair.

Regrettably, as happens in every church and as a result of all evangelistic meetings, not all of those who appeared to respond to the gospel of Christ have continued to live in a way that indicates their desire to serve Him.

For instance, there was Tina. She was the daughter of a local physician but had rebelled against the upper-middle class social life to move in hippie circles. Here she came under the influence of the House of Acts and professed to receive Christ as her Savior. In this fellowship she met and became enamored with Danny Joe.

The two appeared to hit it off well, and since Danny Joe also had acknowledged Christ as his Savior, they asked me if I would perform the wedding ceremony. After several conversations with them, both together and individually, I was convinced that they were not ready for marriage.

While Tina moved as easily in hippie circles as she had in higher society, she still maintained contact with her parents and wished them to be involved in the wedding ceremony. To this, Danny Joe reacted negatively. He wanted no part of the Establishment and consistently rejected the idea of any participation on the part of Tina's family.

Eventually the two drifted apart and, to some extent, up to the present time at least, have not shown a degree of commitment to Christ which those of us who are their friends would like to see.

Pat was another. She had frequented the House of Acts to the point where she understood well the meaning of the gospel of Jesus Christ. One day she spontaneously prayed the sinner's prayer and commited her life to Him. Yet, as we learned later, she continued to live with three fellows, sharing her favors with them indiscriminately. Under pressure from her concerned Christian hippie friends, she finally claimed she had married one of them. But since there has appeared to be no change in her life otherwise, we can only assume that she had not yet made a full commitment to Christ.

During these exciting days we never knew quite what would happen from day to day.

On one occasion the men had brought several people home to the House of Acts from the Living Room. One was a former "Hell's Angel" called "Freddy the Devil" and another a boy known as "Big Tom," who was notoriously unwashed and unkempt. They were warmly welcomed and given food. Bewildered, they listened to the conversations and, I believe even sat in on a Bible study or two. In the process, of course, they were witnessed to by a number of members of the Christian community.

Out on the porch that evening several of the fellows settled into a conversation with them. Freddy dominated the conversation with horrible tales of what he had to do for his "Hell's Angels" initiation. One of the House of Acts men became convinced that the only way these two could be brought to Christ would be through love, and he was having a difficult time showing love for Big Tom because of his filth. Finally he made a decision as to what to do. He got up and left the others. Moments later he returned with a bucket of water and a towel. Solemnly he took of Big Tom's dirty sandals, and washed and dried his feet.

Visibly shaken, Freddy ceased his obscene monologue. "Boys, I'd never do that," he said.

But despite a few unpleasant memories such as these, the tide of spiritual life remained at the full. Although it is difficult to say, perhaps it crested for me at the House of Acts with the Christian hippie wedding described earlier and in the events leading up to it.

twelve

A Romance to Remember

In dealing with young people whom I met at the Living Room and in the House of Acts during those tumultuous years, I have come away with only one overriding impression. That is: neither wealth nor poverty, education or lack of it, parental concern or indifference would ultimately have made the difference in their lives. There appeared to be a larger, more significant force at work which determined the fate of the youth: their lack of knowledge of and commitment to Jesus Christ, the Son of the living God.

If there had been only a few examples, the case would not have been so strong. But with astonishing repetition I saw the results of lives broken and shattered for the lack of this personal relationship to Jesus—and likewise, the astonishing revolution which took place when the Son of God became the Lord of their lives.

One of the most remarkable examples, and at the same time a most typical one, is that of Rick. Born into a conservative Jewish family in Boston on January 24, 1948, Rick had become the victim of his parents' bitter fighting and divorce.

While his father managed his business successfully, he could not discipline his sons. As a result, Rick was put under a psychiatrist's care at an early age because of his rebellion— first to Hebrew school, and later, to public school.

As a fourth grader he had pulled a knife on a girl at school, and the same year he raided the family liquor supply while home for lunch, to return to school drunk.

By the time he was eight, he was smoking and drinking steadily. Later he became a hustler, robbing drugstores and homes and selling the goods to his friends. At thirteen he was taking pills and pushing them, and that same year he was introduced to pot.

By the time Rick reached high school he was full-blown criminal. School authorities tried to help by setting up work-school programs for him, but nothing took effect. At seventeen his mother in desperation allowed him to enlist in the army. But he lasted only nine months, for he was either confined to a stockade or AWOL most of the time. Only family connections finally saved him from a dishonorable discharge.

His army experience gave him a yen to travel. With a friend he robbed a Harvard student of his wallet. With the latter's ID card they secured a driveaway car and took off for Los Angeles. En route the car was badly damaged. They stopped at Barstow, further wrecked the car deliberately, then claimed it had been stolen and abandoned. The insurance company paid off for full repairs, and the young rebels went on to Southern California beaches.

There they engaged in a brisk hustling enterprise, dealing in blank draft cards and drivers' licenses. This was a federal offense, and they were soon apprehended. Rick conned his grandfather into sending one-hundred dollars for the trip back to Boston for the legal counsel that eventually freed him.

Here he got a job at KLH, an electronics manufacturer. At first he liked the image of a working man. Soon, however, he decided that they were all flunkies, and his job became a cover for his hustling talents.

Eventually he was busted for dealing with and possessing illegal drugs.

Again he hit his grandfather for financial help and the services of a good lawyer to save the family name. He was given a light fine and put on probation. The morning when he was due to report to the probation officer he became stoned on acid. Happening across a friend who was about to drive to New York and then on the Middle West, on impulse he skipped out on his probation and went along.

At Bloomington, Indiana, he found a pad with Indiana University students and for six months he played guru for students and faculty children. Here he become involved for the first time with left-wing politics through contacts with Students for a Democratic Society, commonly known as SDS. But this amazingly intelligent boy quickly saw the futility of violence.

It was there that he realized for the first time in his life that he was honestly looking for a spiritual experience rather than a political or social one. He came to see that peace began within the individual, not simply from the society of which he was a part.

Regrettably, his nonviolent inclinations didn't guarantee honesty. Rick got into trouble attempting to forge prescriptions for dope. Hastily he left the community and headed West, financing his travels by hustling stolen merchandise, dope or whatever else he could find. Like a bee to wild honey, he was inexorably drawn to San Francisco and Haight-Ashbury. Here his hustling activities led him to specialize in grass, acid, mescaline and peyote. But not speed or heroin—he had seen too much of those already.

Rick became particularly interested in conversations on spiritual subjects. This was the first time he had found people with whom he could talk intelligently about such matters.

Where to live was no problem. The first night a girl took him to an apartment where she had bedded down the past two nights with a dealer. Rick liked the girl and the layout; he stayed on for a month.

His hustling activities now began to pay off, and he could afford a better apartment; he shared it with a serviceman. Carefully he sorted out from the parade of girls whom he had come to know a slender dark-haired, almond-eyed Chinese named Gloria to be his "old lady." She tidied up the apartment to some extent, prepared meals from time to time, and kept him company at night.

Then, at the height of this crazy mixed-up life, a miracle occurred in Rick's life.

One day he was walking along Haight Street with Gloria when they passed Jack Karman's mission. Attracted by the sign, "Free Coffee and Doughnuts," Rick pulled Gloria inside the door. Here they listened in wide-eyed astonishment as a man described Jesus as "the Lord."

"Ever hear anything like that before?" Rick whispered.

"No." Gloria shook her head.

The two leaned forward, listening intently.

"Your sins will be forgiven by Him if you surrender your lives to Him," the speaker explained.

When the altar call was given, both Gloria and Rick responded. Both knelt before the altar and, as simply and honestly as they knew how repeated the sinner's prayer.

"It was like a bright light shining on my whole life," said Rick. "Not the white light of acid which shows you how naked you are—but the soft enveloping light of the love of Jesus."

Immediately after this experience Rick and Gloria left for Big Sur. Here he spent most of the time reading over and over again the book of John. The Holy Spirit plainly had entered into Rick's mind and heart; his only desire was to saturate himself with the Word of God.

Clearly, he had come to understand forgiveness and that

the burden of his sin had been removed. He hungered for more understanding of the love of God, which amazed him as he turned from page to page.

But his process of spiritual maturity was only beginning. Back at Haight-Ashbury, he soon found the Living Room and threw himself into its fellowship with interest and vigor.

One night he returned to his apartment to find Gloria gone. Neighbors said a group of blacks had raided the apartment, raped Gloria, and taken her with them. Stunned, Rick went to his newfound Christian friends for help. Together the group at the Living Room prayed, and a few hours later Gloria staggered in.

As she sobbed out her story, Gloria admitted to being only seventeen and ready to return home. Her decision was a relief to Rick; the Bible's condemnation of fornication had begun to disturb him. A few days later Gloria returned to her home on the East Coast where she has continued in her walk with the Lord and her witness for Christ.

Now Rick moved into the back room of the Living Room. His pad became his pulpit from which he shared his faith in Christ with all who gave him the opportunity. Patiently he talked with all who would listen—especially with Peter (the fellow mentioned in Chapter One who lived with Megan and Pat), unmindful as he was of Megan's spiritual hunger.

He decided, however, that Pat should stay with Peter and that Megan should leave. For her part, Megan was loath to move—that is, she had been until recently. She had felt appreciated and wanted, and she needed this security. But as Peter's attention to her had increased, she had noticed the growing coolness of Pat.

Moreover, when Rick came around to read the Bible, she noted that the other two weren't really listening. It was the same when Rick brought Ted and Dan and the others to help him. Meanwhile, she was hungry for more knowledge of Jesus Christ, and no one paid any attention to her.

Finally in April of 1968, Megan decided to end the doubtful connubial bliss which had kept her in the community house. She found an old sleeping bag, gathered up her few things, and hitchhiked north to Orgeon. Finding no peace there, she retraced her steps and wound up in Southern California. All along the way she was haunted by the conviction that one way or another she must accept Jesus Christ as her personal Savior and Lord.

A few weeks later, Rick learned her mailing address and wrote Megan a letter. And although nothing was mentioned in the letter, upon reading it Megan had the conviction that she would one day marry Rick. With this in mind she headed back for San Francisco.

Two nights before returning she had her last LSD trip. It proved a rough passage. She dreamed she encountered Satan while walking. In her wild mental wanderings he appeared as a woman who tried to get her to worship Satan instead of Christ. But God's hand was on Megan; she eventually arrived in San Francisco. Eagerly she returned to the circle of her Living Room friends, looking especially for Rick.

But Rick's greeting was casual, and Megan withdrew, hurt and confused. This time she retired to the home of an uncle in Sunnyvale, a suburb of San Francisco, where she spent the next two weeks reading the Bible along with books on Eastern religions. As she persisted, the Holy Spirit focused her attention more and more on the Bible. Finally, totally submissive, she put her faith in Jesus Christ, and the peace of God flooded her soul. With that faith in Christ came freedom from a desire for acid and, in a short time, from pot as well.

A few days afterward Rick called her on the telephone and suggested a camping trip to Northern California with a group of friends. While on this trip Rick proposed marriage. Megan accepted.

* * *

That is how I was asked to perform my first hippie marriage service.

When I think of it now, if the same request had come three years before, I might have turned it down—especially in light of the extenuating circumstances. But already having had the benefit of some of the most rewarding spiritual experiences of my life with these children of our hippie generation, I considered the request a high honor.

I cannot expect all my clergy brethren to agree. Nor do I expect all my brothers in Christ in lay activities of the various churches to understand fully. However, I have related how the Lord has led men—both from His Word and by His Spirit—to this relationship with these newborn children of God.

Of course, I can be wrong. But my conviction is that if we who are called by the name of Christ are to accurately represent Him to the young people of our day, we must understand them better in the environment in which they are living. To do this may mean to accommodate ourselves to situations which we do not always understand or appreciate. But such situations may produce opportunities for witness which we otherwise would never have.

My experience with Rick and Megan is a good example.

Rick continued his witness to his Jewish parents back in Boston. On a trip which Marilyn and I made to the area Rick's charming and well-educated mother called on us. Her concern, of course, was to get a picture of what was really happening to Rick.

"I don't understand it," she repeated again and again.

And I could understand why. His letters were couched in New Testament lauguage:

> Eric Allen Saks, servant of God and of Jesus Christ, to the family in Boston, peace and joy. I write unto you beloved. . . .

That a remarkable change had come to her son, Mrs. Saks could not deny. But her relief was mixed with some apprehension. What kind of a change was it?

"He says he wants to 'save me,' " she said. "What does he mean?"

Carefully Marilyn and I attempted to explain the gospel of Jesus Christ. She appeared grateful, although still obviously perplexed.

"Whatever it is, it must be good. Rick seems so happy," she said.

Moreover, she seemed satisfied, and we left encouraged.

Later Rick's mother visited San Francisco. As she told us later, she wasn't prepared for the hippie attire and the wild mop of hair secured by a headband. Of course, Rick wore no shoes either. (He had given away all such unnecessary accounterments.)

"But when I looked into his eyes, I knew he was different," Mrs. Saks said solemnly.

thirteen

There's Hope Ahead

How to bring to a close my account of what God has done among the young people in the hippie community of San Francisco is not easy. Simply because there is no end.

Perhaps a more sober reason for my hesitation to write before has been an unwillingness to embarrass those of whom I write or their families. Their reassurance that they are willing that the story be told in order that other young people and their parents may be saved the heartache which came to them has been of great encouragement to me.

Above all, the most important reason for producing this record is to provide guidelines for those who will be involved in working with young people in the days ahead. For I am firmly persuaded that the hippie philosophy is a force with which society will be faced for many years to come. Haight-Ashbury as a location is no more the center of true hippie life. Rather, the bright, intelligent young people who had become disenchanted with the Establishment and had the courage to do something about it, negative as that may have been, have now moved on. Some have gone back to the college campus where their impact is being felt in many ways. Here they are demanding a voice in the administration, control over the selection of faculty, and authority in determining of courses. Others are moving into industry, the professions, and government. And with all this, their influence in society overall is almost incomprehensible.

So, what happens to this hippie-oriented individual when he meets Jesus Christ as Savior and Lord becomes of inestimable importance.

Hopefully our experiences will be helpful as well as encouraging. Naturally, as I have already indicated, there have been some disappointments. But Paul finally gave up on Demas. However, even as I recall this, I remember also that heartwarming reference in the same context to John Mark. This young man, who quit so easily while accompanying Paul and Barnabas on their first missionary journey, in time became a profitable worker and, as indicated in 2 Timothy 4:11, an able writer.

Ted and Liz, Dan and Sandy, Lonnie and Connie, Rick and Megan, Steve and Sandi, Jim and Judy—as well as many others—are only beginning to make their impact in the areas and situations of influence into which the Lord is sending them. The marks of maturing insight and responsible action are there to be seen by any fair observer. And it is unjust to write off others who are still in the process of maturing simply because old traits occasionally crop up.

Steve and Sandi and Jim and Judy were the first families to break out of the communal life. Jim, old-time Lutheran that he is, was asked to take a position as a Lutheran youth worker. Thus, it became expedient for him and his family to settle in their own home.

With his training and experience in the field of radio, it was quite natural that Steve should return to his profession of mass communications. Family Stations put him to work in San Francisco first. A year after this move, Steve had the opportunity to move to CBS in New York City. Here he is happy in his occupation and the opportunities for Christian witness which it affords.

Jim is currently director of the Way West Biblical Research Center and he and Judy continue their witness in the Bay area of California.

Dan and Sandy and their two young children are living in an apartment at Golden Gate Theological Seminary where Dan has started as a student. Their move to the nearby seminary has put them in a position to return to active participation in our church. They are most welcome, for such committed, understanding and earnest young adults as they, are what any church needs to help in its ministry to the contemporary world.

Dan's face is a picture of peace and love for people. When I first saw him I would never had forecast such a happy result being possible. That face was etched with lines of misery, clearly revealing the struggle of his years of trying to live without God. Now even his personal grooming has been revolutionized. We knew him for a long time as one who seemed dedicated to a totally casual and even ragged appearance. Sandy shares his testimony in her own warm way. She joins in the church activity and visits and helps her neighbors just as she did in Marin City, opening her heart to numerous women and children.

Ted and Liz and their two children are back in Sausalito, close to the apartment where they once invited many to share the hospitality of hippie life. They rent a house with abundant room and a spacious yard. Ted is working to revive his old sail-making trade and has launched his own private business. He is on call for speaking engagements and travels widely in this part of the country as well as to other parts of the United States.

Ted is an accepted and valuable member of a group of resourceful young men who meet regularly in Palo Alto. They are in demand as teams for spiritual emphasis and related ministries throughout the United States and beyond.

111

Ted also is now serving our church as a member of its board of trustees.

Then there are Megan and Rick.

One day a few months ago they returned to the Bay area from an extended visit in Southern California where they had been carrying on a witnessing program to young people. They drove a converted bakery truck, now decorated with flowers, scrolls, designs—and, of course, Scripture verses. It was loaded with New Testaments and gospel tracts.

They pulled up in front of Dan and Sandy's home in Marin City. Within minutes prowlers broke in the locked van, no doubt expecting to find drugs. Reacting to their disappointment, they rolled the truck down the hill, scattering its contents as it went.

Shouts from the street attracted the attention of those inside the house. Rushing out, they viewed the scene with consternation.

But when they had examined the situation more closely, Rick began to grin. Damage to the car was repairable. Some New Testaments and tracts remained, but those that were scattered were being picked up by the citizens of Marin City—young people and adults alike.

"How else could we have gotten the gospel so well distributed?" Rick asked.

And so it has gone—with these in the inner circle of the Living Room and the House of Acts—as well as with many, many others who made contact only long enough to imbibe of the new life through faith in Jesus Christ. From there they have gone their way, witnessing to the joy and excitement of this life in the Spirit.

In their wake, and in the tradition of the Living Room and the House of Acts, have since come other witnesses to the gospel of Jesus Christ. One interesting development has been the emergence of a number of straight individuals and similarly straight organizations. Adapting their techniques to the mind of the hippie, they have seen a good response to their approach.

112

However, looking at the scene from the point of view of a pastor and his church, I would have to admit that some churches and ministers are definitely more open to this kind of ministry than others. Strong concern and commitment appear more likely to be found in individuals rather than in whole fellowships. Well aware of the complete metamorphosis through which I myself had to go, I am loath to judge. At the same time, when I hear some of my colleagues assert that our churches had better learn to deal with the philosophy represented by the hippie movement or they will fail almost totally in reaching the young people of the next generation, I am inclined to agree.

At the moment, it appears to me that among evangelical churches a certain polarization is taking place. At one extreme is what could be called "fortress" churches. By taking a strong stand for faithfulness to the Bible and an equally strong refusal to become involved in new ministries, such churches have become entrenched. This is, plainly, a safe and sure policy. Here disenchanted members of other churches, of all shades of theology, can retreat to a refuge where they can defend themselves against all assaults—including the hippie philosophy.

At the other pole are churches committed to projecting the gospel of Christ into the confused world of today through new and effective techniques. Those of us who are struggling with this approach also are as committed to the same gospel as those who choose the fortress stance. But to reach the modern man, we are convinced that we must take some risks; and we know we are bound to make some mistakes. The translations of the Scriptures which we employ are not always approved by the most conservative. The music we use often sounds garish and, to some, unchristian. Admittedly, not everyone can worship serenely in such an atmosphere.

But I do thank God for those who read the challenge as I do, and are willing to accept the change.

We pastors of churches in transition—particularly where

the hip generation is involved—find ourselves continually in the middle, trying to minister in two directions and hoping to see a real joining of hands and hearts. I cannot feel, as some of my colleagues apparently do, that the churches we serve are hopeless. I cannot see myself dropping this "bag of old dry bones" to get out where the action is. I grant there is a large degree of resistance to action within the churches. But this only means that we have a job to do, and I am convinced that God has many people with great potential and spiritual power in these churches, through whom He can and will work.

Again and again Marilyn and I have found ourselves pleading with both sides (fortress and transition) to be more understanding, more aware of each one's own stubbornness, and more willing to forbear. There have been abundant offenses on both sides. But nothing is more clear to me after these years of standing between two groups than the fact that no one is perfect.

Moreover, it is my observation that young persons affected by the hippie philosophy also harbor emotional problems. Indeed, I have been led to conclude that emotional problems breed the hip philosophy. I think I have recognized many symptoms of longtime emotional illnesses, in varying degrees of severity, among these young people.

But even when such problems are spotted and attempts made to gently lead needy persons into helpful counsel, another barrier rears itself. As representatives of the Establishment, we are suspect; hence, our influence often is limited.

Happily, with the hippie's awareness to mysticism, he is likely to identify many of the so-called mental disorders as actual demons or, at least, demon attacks. And with his thorough knowledge of the Scriptures, and the scriptural approach to demoniac activity so clearly illustrated in the Bible, he often handles the problem through exorcism.

If this always were the answer to the problem, we might have come to a solution much sooner. Regrettably, in my opinion, it is not so. I continue to believe that there is great

114

need also for genuine Christian mental therapists in the church today. Emotional illness is hardly limited to hippies.

The important thing for us to remember, I believe, is that hippies, the now generation—call them what you will—have been turned off by self-proclaimed experts. At the top of the success add in today's world, young people see phony figures and a great deal of futility. Their judgments are not all fair; they do need some professional help. Many of their suggestions make no more sense than the culture they condemn. But I have found them responsible to God's good news about Jesus Christ when offered with a common touch. To me this means that ordinary Christians and ordinary churches *can* reach them.

We common followers of Jesus can be instruments of—to use an old but effective term—*revival.* This will depend upon our willingness to make some changes. We shall need to be very patient. We shall have to let novices say some hard things about us. We must recognize that some will judge us unfairly and criticize us unjustly. We shall also need to recognize that some of the criticism will be fair, simply because we will make mistakes.

Perhaps more than anything else, we shall have to think in terms of "we" rather than of "we" and "they." In other words, we shall need very much to be reminded that *we are all sinners,* and that God has been amazingly gracious to receive any one of us.

It is a terrible mistake, but a common practice, for Christians to think that clean, courteous, cultured people are more lovable to God than the cruder, sometimes dirty, creatures of society.

Today the voice of the hippie is being heard in the. land. Tomorrow that now feeble cry may have been amplified into a mighty roar.

If the past years of experience have taught me anything, they have enabled me to believe that Jesus Christ alone is the answer to all men's needs—no matter what their backgrounds may be.

fourteen

Postscript

If the preceding record were all that had resulted from the House of Acts, I would still have great cause to thank God for allowing me to participate in what He was doing. But there has been much more. The House of Acts itself was truly only the beginning. Even as I have been writing, reports come to me of new Christian communes springing up —not only in California, but in many other parts of the United States. The Lord is plainly moving in a truly marvelous way in bringing young men and women together to share their common faith in Jesus Christ through community action.

But this is not all.

So great appears to be the hunger on the part of youth that the message of the gospel—presented in a variety of different ways, some even in the traditional "straight" method— is receiving wide acceptance.

As members of Evangelical Concerns share a sense of the gracious divine purpose which worked quietly in our midst through those early years, we can now see more clearly that individuals have been brought together, experiences have been gained leading to a maturing insight, faith has been strengthened, convictions reinforced—all leading to the emergence of a thrilling, satisfying, broad gospel thrust into the heart of hippiedom.

Early in 1969, Dan reported that he had met a group of Christians working out of a rallying point called Soul Inn. This place operated in connection with a tiny Southern Baptist mission church, Lincoln Park Church, of which the Rev. Al Gossett was pastor. Kent Philpot, a student at Golden Gate Seminary (Southern Baptist) in Mill Valley whom the men had met in the Haight-Ashbury section, had become active at Soul Inn.

Although Kent was a college graduate, his background included the beatnik scene. While in the air force he began to sense the hopelessness of the life he was living and from time to time visited the First Baptist Church of Fairfield with his wife, Bobbie. She received Christ as her Savior two years before Kent. Finally becoming convinced that there was no other hope except in Christ, Kent acknowledged Him as his Lord.

Upon entering seminary Kent was curious to discover if he could present the gospel to Haight-Ashbury hippies so that they would respond. He went into the area and began to talk to people. On his second day he met a fellow named Dave, who he learned was something of a "big wheel" in Haight.

Dave was caretaker of the local Hindu temple and was well versed in Hindu rights and lore. Kent arranged with him to conduct Bible studies in the temple basement. This led to Dave's conversion and he moved out of the temple to live with the Philpots. The two young men became an effective team as they witnessed for Christ. For Dave's background of many years of dope addiction, lawlessness, and a stretch in the state penitentiary gave him a voice of authority on the street.

118

Soon the same problem that plagued us at the Living Room came to haunt Kent and Dave: Where could they provide shelter for young hippies who were responding to their witness for Christ?

A seminary student friend, Al Gossett, gave a sympathetic ear. So did Dr. Francis DuBose of the seminary faculty and a member of Gossett's Lincoln Park church. The church members subsequently voted to establish Soul Inn as a temporary refuge, while a part of the church's facilities served for sleeping and eating quarters. Into this work were drawn other seminary students such as Oliver Heath and Paul Bryant, both coming from strong Christian homes and both genuine straights like Gossett and DuBose.

In the meantime Kent had discovered the Living Room. Gradually he and his associates became acquainted and began to feel at ease with our staff. They visited the House of Acts, and the fabric of their lives came to be woven more and more closely together. These fellows were not also interested in the gifts and dedication of David Best, a fine young artist. Best was married to the sister of the girl whom Dave met at the House of Acts and later married.

This entire group of young men was meeting and praying together, Dan told me, with an idea of forming some kind of cooperative organization for ministering to youth. Dan and Ted had told them about our involvement in Evangelical Concerns and of our similar interests. Eventually a meeting was arranged. To me the experience was refreshing and stimulating.

Could these be the new breed of Christian workers whom the Lord is raising up in our day? I asked myself, looking around at the eight or ten young men and women in the room. They certainly didn't look like the usual Sunday school-teacher type with whom I had been acquainted in the past few years. *Perhaps He is teaching me another one*, I reasoned.

As I look back now, perhaps it was that night that I

realized in a new way that I was seeing a new and different generation. With enlightened eyes I saw them as deeply concerned, committed, Spirit-filled men and women. That didn't mean that they were altogether wise or able to conquer the whole world for Christ overnight. It did mean, however, that they had a vision and a capability for a type of ministry for which the institutional straight such as I was simply not prepared.

As a matter of fact, Zion's Inn for Girls had already been established by Kent and Dave and their wives in the big home which once had served as the House of Acts. Zion's Inn provides a haven for single girls needing a refuge from the life that has proved so sad a delusion.

Now another strong agency has joined the family of the committed. Only months ago Jack Sparks, Pat Matrisciana, Fred Dyson and their wives and families came to Berkeley to attempt an evangelical ministry among students and street people. They are straights drawn to the colorful life of hip society out of natural interests and genuine concern.

Jack Sparks is a veteran university professor holding a Ph.D. degree. Pat Matrisciana is an ordained Baptist minister. Fred Dyson, not currently able to participate directly in the project, is a businessman. All had worked together in Campus Crusade for Christ.

Their highest hopes have been exceeded in the Christian World Liberation Front. Their presence in the university area, at first received with distrust or great reservation, has become the center of another revolution.

Informal gatherings, Bible studies, and serious intellectual dialogues have multiplied so fast and with such results that it must be called an explosion. A San Francisco newsman has characterized the organization as "the most militant currently on the University of California Berkeley Campus."

This is a true, unembarrassed, biblical Christian witness. Perhaps that has something to do with its success in the wake of other disappointing efforts in Berkeley. But also to be

120

credited is the *modus operandi* of the staff. They have used their God-given intelligence for learning to communicate with the street people. They wear casual clothing, sport moderately long hair and trim beards. They take advantage of all the communications media available.

Using funds provided by interested supporters, they are producing their own translations of New Testament portions in language understandable to their congregation—carefully rendered to preserve the Word of God as it was given. They hold to the full authority and inspiration of the Bible. Jesus is designated "Liberator and Leader" in place of "Savior and Lord."

Their approach is to produce cleverly made-up and illustrated booklets and leaflets. Among them is one offering health advice to their constituents. It is called *People's Medical Handbook* and explains that it is published by the Christian Revolutionary Medical Committee. By way of introduction it asks, "Where is your head?" The copy that follows is equally provocative:

> We are part of a cultural revolution. The whole world scene is changing—from the youth up. Most of us have turned the materialism gig down. We are building new life styles and a revolutionary culture. To do it right, we need to know how to keep our minds and bodies going strong without having to turn to the establishment. That is what this pamphlet is all about.
>
> Everything from nutrition to keeping your head straight is in it. Everything is here to serve the people in the name of Jesus. Read it and live. Power to the people! Power through Jesus! All power through the Spirit!

The booklet explains how people short on cash can live on a healthy diet for as little as ninety cents a day. It gives detailed advice on food values, menus, eating habits, then on bodily hygiene and first aid, with warnings in low key on drugs of all common kinds. And all of this comes with a simple and intelligent word about how it all relates to Christ.

In addition, a well-edited newspaper *Right On*, an underground radio, public rallies on the famed steps of Sproul Hall, with testimonies by newly won converts, form the impressive front of this new revolution.

Every event that draws youth—such as the wild demonstrations against institutions of higher learning or the Vietnam war, or the fantastic mass of youth and autos that jammed hillsides at Altamont Speedway when the Rolling Stones appeared there—finds an army of CWLF youth on hand.

They cleverly exploit every opportunity to witness.

At Altamont Speedway, when thousands of cars with their occupants were waiting for hours for their turn to drive out, members handed out their revolutionary-appearing brand of gospel tracts.

Some of the group helped stop a fight. Then, to the interested crowd packed closely around, one of them spoke out, "I guess you wonder why I have called you all together today..." and he went on to describe the one revolutionary leader who could give them life and a worthy cause—Jesus. Many appeared to profess Christ as the result of his witness.

One of the provocative leaflets used by the organization is titled *And After This War?* The copy challenges the students in a language which they understand:

> As participants in contemporary events, people tend to be restricted by the limited prospective of the immediate situation. Fifty years earlier you see the great war to end all wars—a prediction we can safely criticize as naive.
>
> The question, then, "Why have violent conflicts continued to plague mankind throughout history, despite numerous and varied system changes? Will a Utopian economy and political system eradicate the seemingly inescapable stigma of social and psychological struggle?" The people in China or Czechoslovakia are no closer to that ideal world than we are in

122

America. In fact, as history insists, no kind of environment guarantees that we will finally realize the beautiful society we so desperately want. It should be obvious—something is wrong with us! The great cop out today is to blame some impersonal institution or system.

Jesus proclaimed a spiritual revolution to bring about a fundamental change within, to deal with the faulting components of every system—the human components. Accept Him as your liberator and leader; then join others of His heavenly family here to change this world.

RADICALIZE THE REVOLUTIONARY MOVEMENT! GET INTO THE WORLD'S GREATEST REVOLUTION!

The Christian World Liberation Front obviously is no more perfect than any other Christian organization, no matter how noble its purpose. I find some cases of offensiveness or of misunderstanding of the Front's character and objectives. Not surprisingly, there are breaches in communication between them and some of the more established community. Undoubtedly there is fault on both sides. And it all sounds familiar to me. Give them time. After a while some rough edges will be smoothed off, some hostility to Establishment will soften—and unfortunately some bad connections will become worse. But God will work in spite of the problems.

But the youth scene constantly explodes in all directions, and the variety of fireworks still blows my mind.

The final phase of preparing this story for publication coincides with the opening of a Christian Free University in San Francisco. It is the brain child of Kent Philpot and an enthusiastic core of his associates. As with other free universities operating in the world of far-out youth, this one provides bonafide learning completely free of charge to students.

The delineating characteristic of this school is that it is

dedicated to teaching the truth grounded in Jesus Christ, in the Word which is God's supernatural revelation to men. The program calls for a one-year basic curriculum with three ten-week quarters. Instruction is offered in Old and New Testament Survey, Church History, Missions and Evangelism, Introduction to Christian Theology, and English. There is little sophistication in curriculum, campus or faculty. But like so many other facets of this strange new world, it may turn out to be the kind of development born of God to help keep the truth alive.

These developments are bound to encourage us. But we have not forgotten the days, not so long ago, when we sometimes wondered aloud if we were actually going *any-where*. My account of early experiences, of trying to get along with converts, is a clear reminder that I wasn't always persuaded that pot heads and acid heads could be sufficiently changed to become responsible Christians.

But God has clearly demonstrated otherwise.

And I am sure that with these and the other organizations—which probably even now are in existence, and the many more which will spring up in the days to come—will be used by God to bring young people to Himself. God is more gracious than we are. The road to destruction is broad and many are taking it. The path to life eternal is narrow, but those who follow it—no matter what their background may be, from the harlots of Jesus' day to the pot heads of our day—are welcome. Jesus simply asks that they commit themselves fully to Him.

And our mission as individuals—whether laymen or ministers—is the same. We simply bear testimony to the fact that this is indeed life—more abundant, and eternal.